Lantern Tree

Lantern Tree is a sensory feast, made up of four riveting collections of poetry.

Chris Baron's *Under the Broom Tree* takes us on a series of awe-filled, expansive, spiritual journeys, whether they occur in domestic spaces or in Mecca. Eastern, Western, and aesthetic beliefs collide in this stunning and contemplative collection that invites us to restore our faith in the magical powers of language, to listen deeply to a poet who speaks carefully, thoughtfully "in muted prayers sewn into me through countless afternoons."

Heather Eudy's *Bills of Lading* documents her extensive travels throughout the United States and Mexico. Eudy invites readers to consider poems as archeological, geographical, and sensual. This is a lush, evocative collection that explores both internal and external landscapes. This is also a daring, erotically-charged collection in which "topless" boys "acquire their own beltless romance" under the speaker's hungry gaze.

The earth itself comes alive in Cali Linfor's *A Book of Ugly Things*. In the poet's hands, a Matilija poppy flower becomes a "native showgirl" and the sky is transformed into a "blue tendon." The ugly is made beautiful again in Linfor's startling, painterly collection, particularly in her provocative sequences that push beyond easy answers. This is vivid imagery with a bite.

The feverish poems in Sabrina Youmans' *Pacific Standard Time* reveal an emotional boldness in which nameless men are counted up like conquests and compared to food: tart cherries, mangoes, and "hot radish heat." These are uneasy poems, poems of unrest, of wound, that depict the fracture of families and histories in lines that seem to rise off the page with their vibrancy, and speak.

—Hadara Bar-Nadav, Author of *A Glass of Milk to Kiss Goodnight* and *The Frame Called Ruin*

Lantern Tree

Four Books of Poems

Chris Baron

Heather Eudy

Cali Linfor

Sabrina Youmans

SD
CWP

SAN DIEGO
CITY WORKS
PRESS

ISBN 978-0-9837837-1-8
Library of Congress Control Number: 2012939332

San Diego City Works Press is a non-profit press, funded by local writers and friends of the arts, committed to the publication of fiction, poetry, creative nonfiction, and art by members of the San Diego City College community and the community at large. For more about San Diego City Works Press please visit our website at cityworkspress.org.

San Diego City Works Press is extremely indebted to the American Federation of Teachers, Local 1931, without whose generous contribution and commitment to the arts this book would not be possible.

Cover Design: Rondi Vasquez
Cover Photo: Andrew Peck
Production Editor: Will Dalrymple | Layout & Editing | willdalrymple.com

Published in the United States by San Diego City Works Press, California

Printed in the United States of America

Contents

Introduction

As readers of poetry, we know we are on a journey, led by a poet's very words, along with images, sounds, and form—the maps that guide us. So we pay attention to the title words *Lantern Tree*, curious to know if such a tree lives in our natural world or, perhaps, exists in the imagination of a poet and will be the inspiration for the other poets or us as readers. The word lantern is evocative. It is a word that begins in our mouths with a lilting "l"—our tongues gently touching the back of our top front teeth. There is a rhythm and beat as we let our mouths and tongues tap out the word, its softness and warmth. Lantern seems a word from another time, a time when light burned yellow and with a glow. In the days of lanterns, people's lives were shorter—there were life-threatening sicknesses we have cures for today and hardships for which we now have conveniences. Days were shorter—for many, nights meant darkness, for it required money and labor to keep a lantern burning, a fireplace heating, a candle lit. Lantern is an ancient word. Its etymology suggests its journey back and back, from French to a Latin text of John XVIII to Greek. Lantern means a case for carrying a light. From ancient Greece the definitions "light torch" and "horn" complete the meanings of the two-syllable word lantern. The second part of lantern came from the Greek word that stood for horn. Animal horns were sometimes used for the sides of the case that fitted around the flaming light. So we readers investigate the sound, the meaning, and any messages we are given about the title words of the book we are about to take our first step into, and we do have a message from the four poets. We are told, "The lantern tree acknowledges that many hands are needed to assemble the possibility of light." Even so, the poets remind us "each book is a thing of its own, has a mouth and tongue of its own, makes and unmakes a home of its own." Hence we breathe in the full title: *Lantern Tree: Four Books of Poems*.

Lantern Tree: Four Books of Poems shines its light on the separate paths of San Diego poets Chris Baron, Heather Eudy, Cali Linfor, and Sabrina Youmans. Their footwork—four books of poetry—guides us into their worlds. Readers follow up a dusty, stony trail, through a weeded, shadowed lot, off an asphalt road, down tangled, blackened embankment. Sometimes we travel alongside speakers stepping into borrowed cars, buses, and trains, chasing down the last light. Some board jets, cross state lines, country borders, seeking connection, fleeing connection. Other times we stumble in desert bright light. We learn that light does not always illuminate. It can blind, blotting out what eyes seek. Still, light can be transformative. Perhaps by chance or charm, an ancient guide might lead us through a city, where people are bound by sidewalks, roads, and cement-lined culverts to a tree, a living thing from the natural world, its branches dipping and beckoning with lanterns. In Youmans' poem "The Tribe Ignites," magic is possible, for in this poem a lamp becomes a chime "that rings / the awareness / .... Each transparent globe, / baring within a story, / a meaning burning with the / intention of interaction." And like the lanterns, each of the *Lantern Tree* poets shines with a story, an image, a ringing inside. They invite us to risk interacting with their poems.

In making the connection with the poets, we readers receive the unspoken promise of kinship—with another who has survived the crises of spirit, mind, and body and who has found the words to speak about life's mysteries. To live in extreme is a struggle, not light or darkness, but to live in what Linfor calls "more complex mixed states of being," we can hope to learn something about "two things being true at once" and "come to an acceptance of ugly things," that life is not about always feeling safe, held and loved, a part of, but often is about knowing fear, feeling abandoned, being called ugly and no good, and being alone. As humans we seek beyond ourselves, we reach past our imperfect families, travel beyond our familiar roads, towns, and countries. We seek spiritual life beyond what we know, reframing childhood religious upbringings, casting them off at times and finding balance in nature or acceptance in new ways of being.

When readers connect with the poet and speaker through the moments each poet gives us, there is a gift for readers in that embodied in these poems real life is mirrored: loss can be pure loss. For in the next moment of loss, there may be something less than pure loss on the continuum, even a gift.

Early on in their discussion of what they hoped their book would offer, Baron, Eudy, Linfor, and Youmans recognized that "the poems lean against each other for support and weave the light and the darkness in a quest for purpose, family, community, and reason." Readers will discover, as the poets themselves did as they worked on their book, that they were meant to bring their books—their individual life stories—together; for these poets are connected as seekers, as travelers and pilgrims, examining their faith—whether in family, friends, lovers, nature, or their spirituality. These poets will lead readers through interesting poetic forms, including the longer meditation poems that allow them and us to explore facets of the hardest questions of many of our lives—what it means to be able to return to the self, whether in relationships with others or oneself; what it means to trust again after childhood betrayals; what it means to become aware, accept, and hope. Readers will see connections between the poets in nature—trees, clouds, and bodies of water become mediums to explore adaptation and personal survival. Real darkness—the night sky, a tunnel, a tangled, covered ravine—and light—lanterns, lamps, candles and sunlight—all with metaphoric power will be explored and celebrated. And above all else, individually, "Each poet responds to the beauty, the truth, and the ugliness found along the way."

Lantern Tree opens with Chris Baron's book *Under the Broom Tree*. Baron leads with a startling poem, "The Language of Rivers," that tempts the eye with its shape and pleases the ear with compelling phrasings and occasional internal rhymes as when we are asked what it might be like "to flow into a widening mouth of salt and blue / no stagnant pools just the cold and constant push of every moment." The reader may hear an echo of Ralph Waldo Emerson in a line, "how long until you put your ear to the flow / allow yourself a chance to believe . . ." and Walt Whitman with the intimate "you" address and invitation to visit the river every day, to get out of the car and be in your body on the water's edge so that from your sandwich you can "pull off the crusts feed silvery fish swimming." We, too, are pushed out of our comfort zone as readers who cannot help but ponder the same haunting questions that the speaker is asked in the poem: "Does the water listen?" And when we are told that there is "just the cold and constant push of every moment," it is a starkly beautiful reminder that reality is in the now, the present.

Throughout Baron's poetry, words from sacred texts, admired thinkers, and the poet's own gifted choosing are crucial to the experience of reading *Under the Broom Tree.* Through the repetition of key words such as hands, water, lion, light, and breath, ideas and struggles take on layered nuances and more complex dimension. In the opening poem, "The Language of Rivers," and throughout the book, the concept of stasis versus change is explored in phrasings referring to stagnation and waiting, in contrast to being open to the flow and to taking "a chance to believe." The river motif is explored, turned over, and meditated upon until the reader recognizes the possibility that "The Language of Rivers" may be the poet struggling with his sense of what is divine and what is expected of him. Bodies of water, whether rivers or oceans, become emblematic places where the body, mind, and spirit are tested in Baron's poems.

Baron describes his book as "a personal journey from childhood to adulthood." An early synopsis about Baron's book describes how adulthood has offered Baron "a rediscovery of the self and a making of his own journeys as an athlete, a husband, a traveler, and a father." Further, "The search for a transformed self has forced him to walk a physical and spiritual path, confronting the truth of his beliefs set against the strong pull of family history and cultural heritage." Stylistically, Baron, like his sister poets Linfor and Eudy, finds narrative form useful in exploring themes that take the reader back through time and also place the reader alongside struggling speakers in poems. As well as a narrative poet, Baron is an imagistic poet, who in this collection relies primarily on "free verse with some use of syllabics for control."

Among the many poets he admires, Baron says he continues to be influenced by poet Philip Levine—someone who presents in honest, sometimes gritty detail the lives of everyday workers and family members—and who writes from a strong, male voice, a trait readers will admire in Baron's work. In "The Seedplanter," Baron describes the seedplanter's fingers as "blocks of iron" and later wonders "how many seeds / the iron blocks have planted." He tells us the man gives up his seat while his little daughter sleeps. Baron honors the simple, generous gestures of strangers in his poems. Further, narrative allows Baron to take his readers on his journey right to the place, present or past, and as our guide, he shows us what he sees—witness to life on the streets of New York or Jerusalem or Jericho. He credits Carolyn Forché, her craft and her courage, in showing him how to not just give details of a particular moment, but to expand and complicate it with social and historical context, whether in New York naming the subway stops, in the museum naming the atrocities done to a people he names and belongs to, or in Israel or in a bus or taxi at the border witnessing the same things the others do. The poems that speak to Baron's spiritual searching and his journey to Israel will show the reader the powerful influence of the Israeli poet Yehuda Amichai, a man who inspires Baron to write about the dry land and outstretched hands he greets. Amichai challenges Baron to write about the complex subject of what to call home, how to live a centered life. Baron says, "I am telling my story the best way I know . . . poems have always been the way for me to articulate and understand events, experiences, and emotions that are beyond my own humanity—divine moments in some sense."

Childhood unfolds in the personal, narrative poems "Field Trip" and "Still Life" as we witness his earlier experiences being raised by a free-spirited artist. With strong female figures such as his flamboyant mother as well as his salt of the earth grandmother who in "Origins" acts out the cutting and stacking of wheat, their Romanian family's means of survival, as she ". . . swung her arm / up and down, until the spatula / scratched the ceiling," Baron learned early to not just be proud of his heritage but to be a storyteller who in his grandmother's words would let others know "this is how we did it!" And those very words resonate as we read on in "Dog Hill" when in New York at a museum, it is now Baron's father who, he says, "shows me 'Holocaust,' / fills in maps empty until now / . . . cups his hands around my face, / whispers, 'never again.' . . ." Baron reveals that he sees the fragile beauty of words, and in lines reminiscent of a respected contemporary poet Li-Young Lee, Baron writes of the beauty of ". . . cities beneath cities, morning snow, / and returning home."

Within narrative, by building metaphors and images, Baron subtly, yet with powerful effect, reveals the internal struggle of a young boy. "Central Park Zoo" begins with a resonating quote by Daniel Quinn, "If you can't understand what's keeping you in, the will to get out soon becomes confused and ineffectual." A subtle tie is quickly made in the opening stanza between the baby gorilla and the young boy who has begun his admiration of the natural world, animal life and the "autumn sun." Yet the trip to the zoo with his parents is not an easy one; in the second stanza it is as if the poet is a painter, whose brushwork images present a portrait of a son caged between his parents, a mother whispering an oft-repeated story in one ear while a father ". . . remained distant, / smoking on a bench, / already looking past his / seven-year-old boy." The speaker tells the reader that before long he will grow in awareness as now the lion paces, seals swim laps, and most poignantly, ". . . the silverback rested his head on the cold bars / . . . toward the light and air / unable to comprehend his own question." The reader remembers the opening quote, and although the speaker states, "I too began to look for a way out," he is still young and in his struggle to understand his family, his religious roots, the pull of human desire—his attraction to girls and his testing of his own physical strength as a young athlete—he will have to wander and stumble through his confusion and admit his own ineffectualness into his early manhood.

One of the strengths, in addition to Baron's honesty and invitation to accompany him on his passage through childhood, is the poet's ability to clearly craft an image and resist adorning it with any words that present commentary or overstep beyond his own perception; the gorilla is not anthropomorphized in a way that is not real or begs our sympathy. In other poems, such as "The Seedplanter," we are told that a man's eyes are "luminous" and in view of the speaker but also that the seedplanter's gaze may just as likely be out the window. No image or subject is accidental in a poem. As the speaker comes to terms with his own awareness sharpening, he lets illusions drop, as he "found that the gorilla house was only a box / of metal . . ." and later in "The Green Box," the speaker "wondered how the green box / would find us when we moved." Although painful to realize the reality of animal cages and promised but unsent gifts—"Promises are impossible for you"—the poet learns to speak his truth, ". . . that was the closest / I could ever come to you." Learning what to do with broken trust and the push-pull desire of being with another and being strong alone with one's own hands and spirit are central concepts in Baron's poems. Baron, like his sister poets, presents speakers struggling with perception of connection to others.

Emerging manhood, connection and disconnection in love relationships, disintegration and survival are explored in a series of poems that begins with "Summer" and ends with "Absolution." Water is the medium in which desire, strength, and connection are tested in this grouping. In "Summer," the male speaker is the one who waits and admits he never felt safe while the remembered girl, in sundress and pigtails, jumps first. Perhaps in a young boy's emerging desire for a girl—"floating backwards, / calling me, splashing, laughing"—he develops the courage to jump, to break the move, not stagnate. We will meet the girl again in other poems of Baron's book; is she emblematic of fear or temptation? Readers will have to continue on with the poet's journey to the final poem of his book. Baron extends the use of water imagery at the end of the poem when the speaker still hears the girl's voice "smooth as river-rock, / gentle as water-glass." Here the connection to the girl is positive for her voice is recalled when the speaker is "at the edge of things."

In "Waking the Boats," water is the medium again with the speaker, one of a crew team, awakening his own body along with readying the boats. Baron skillfully uses alliteration and detail in phrases that praise the body and practice in examples such as "loosening our long limbs" and "stretching sinewy muscle." Verbs are active as in "shift" and "unhitch." The descent closer to water serves as a metaphor for an action that is true and also can resonate with the speaker's struggle to see himself clearly for long: "Lowering the boats gently, / . . . we climb into the shell / so near the water, / our reflections disappear."

In the following poem, "Other Women and Oars," a poem delivered mostly in couplets, the speaker opens with a singular line, declaring, "This isn't my life. Nothing here is mine." What follows are couplets detailing the disconnection and distance between the couple. Water is in the picture with the woman soaking herself with a hose and other references include water "racing down gutters," puddles, and the haunting image of "the damp indentation of a curled body" in the bed. In contrast to the speaker's feeling of discomfort, powerlessness, and a lack of control in his relationship, there are the speaker's claims that he knows water, "the comfort of a body almost weightless, the impossibility of control, / the power of bodies that skim its surface." As the two lovers become more distant, the speaker continues to detail in extended imagery the connection of the rowers: "The lifting boat, the crush of water, once eight now one, the boat lifting / the glide on the water, the drag disappears, flight." The language and effect are both powerful and beautiful. The poem does not end in a tone of despair. The speaker lists moves he's begun to make: he's moved the bed, cleaned the desk, and learned to boil rice. In a solitary line that closes the poem, he admits he's isolated himself, but in doing that he claims, "My hands are again my own." His hands are linked to manly strength. He trusts them when he rows. He is learning to be okay with being alone again. He has returned to the self.

Moving from the medium and imagery of water to the environment of a vehicle—be it bus or train—Baron, like other poets such as Eudy, explores concepts of connection and disconnection, personal disintegration and spiritual awakening. Other poets such as Youmans have speakers boarding trains and finding patterns of connection through awareness of light and darknesses, clouds seen through windows, while the poet Linfor also explores light and darkness as her speakers confront painful events involving betrayal, death, and birth. Baron's "Absolution" is a long, sectioned poem that tracks a crisis for a speaker who grabs a train, and within the flashing interior light notices the words "me" scratched into a portrait of Absolut Vodka. The poet makes a stylistic move as the speaker makes the words his own and reminds readers that other people's words—even those scratched on public property—pass through us, surround us, and that we are connected to the language and words of others not present, from the past and possibly into eternity. The speaker breaks down as the ride continues, feeling the "weight of my own decisions" pushing him down like "giant awkward hands" naming them as "a heaviness of mistakes and time spent." In his own suffering, he is able to see another man "breaking down" and "on one knee now," yet the speaker doesn't embellish what he witnesses but admits, "I can't tell if he is laughing or crying or praying."

Expanded imagery, and most importantly, the speaker's awareness and the poet's interpretation of the motifs of darkness and light are offered in the "Kings Highway" section, the second to last, and then the final section, "Avenue P" of "Absolution." "Kings Highway" opens with the speaker pleading, "Rescue me / because here I am now alone." In the poems of all four of the poets of *Lantern Tree,* speakers sometimes desire and strive to be alone, to stand strong on their own, while other times this same state can be perceived by speakers as one to be feared, one to be avoided at all costs, or one that may have a stigma attached to it as being unacceptable or unlovable. The speaker says he is waiting—something we have seen other speakers do in Baron's poems—and he adds that he is waiting to "get to where it isn't dark." The reason is elaborated upon and in that expansion Baron links with the other poets in the book who build on the metaphor of the lantern and light, something that one can make true statements about in terms of its earthly or universal properties but, above all else, a symbol emblematic of creation and connection beyond our human imaginations. The speaker offers, "A light in a dark place cannot comfort itself—it needs other lights, / like the galaxies . . . beautiful vortexes spinning . . . / and they don't let up until they are full of stars / packed with the power of creation and destruction. . . ." Out of the speaker's despair, he seems to have had an awakening, an awareness of life forces bigger than himself. He claims, "We are galaxies, filled with swirling, light and luminous bodies. We attract other bodies into our / orbit as we move." And in the midst of his realization, he repeats, "Rescue me," for now he wants to be connected as he announces, "I am closer now than ever before." In "Avenue P," the light streaming through the window forces the speaker to close his eyes, yet he must still make his request, "Rescue me," for in asking, he humbles himself for absolution.

Further poems are enriched by the motif of light and darkness as well as continuing to center around the connection—and—disconnection theme as the poet explores religion, particularly his Jewish upbringing and how it has shaped his identity. The opening lines of "Making Aliyah" remind readers that Baron is not just a wordsmith, but also a philosopher: "Because we can think / we are afraid of the dark." From the platform of the opening observation, Baron launches the reader back to moments in time when the speaker as a young man tried on religious rituals and traditions, and more in his attempt to become a devoted son of his God; and all of the practice is necessary preparation for the speaker as he becomes an adult who is still searching and trying to keep his promise—a promise to go to Israel.

In prose form, we read that the young Jewish speaker gets down from his bunk, and perhaps from the influence of TV, he prays like a Christian but knows "Jewish kids don't pray like this," and later at 13, when called to the Torah, he "speaks in muted prayers sewn . . . through countless afternoons with the Rabbi." Once again we have a speaker who waits, "I wait for manhood to come over me," he tells us, though he's distracted by women upstairs and other sensations. The speaker is honest in his hope for some "change to happen, some touch from the almighty, something to make it true," and readers from many religions with adult initiation rites that all young must go through to make public their commitment to their religion will recognize the true feelings of this speaker. Still, this young man, this speaker, makes a serious promise to go to Israel, perhaps not realizing that he has a calling to become a pilgrim, to join a long line of people who have made pilgrimages to the Holy Land throughout the ages.

"Making Aliyah" is an important centerpiece poem in Baron's book for it gives the reader moments in the development of a person who reveals his human desires while striving for a spiritually centered life. Earlier poems in Baron's book have been leading us to "Making Aliyah," and readers feel like we know this speaker. He is a boy becoming a man. He is learning about bodily desire. In some ways his ineffectual wandering is given a feminine aspect as he claims, "She demands I follow her into hidden places, wander for years." He goes on to admit, "I spend my reality on her." The poet is continuing to deepen the mystery of who "she" really represents, and by the book's end we realize that Baron has been bringing us closer to Elijah's story of the broom tree all along.

The poet shows the speaker a boy experiencing his desire with girls, but repeats a line we've heard in an earlier poem: "this isn't my life." He seems to be struggling with the balance of being human with instincts, yet questing for spiritual meaning. Another snapshot features the speaker with a woman, drinking wine and doing revisionist interpretations of Biblical stories and beliefs. In yet another prose section, the speaker is experimenting with a myriad of practices from different belief systems: "One foot toward Mecca, one foot in the temple, one hand folded over prayer beads, the other in an open meditation." In the midst of the listing of practices he admits, "My mind is unfastened to the loudest voice." Strong, universal images of hands, sunlight, roots, seeds, and paths enforce and enlarge the explanation leading up to the speaker's recognition that he is ready to keep a promise, to make his pilgrimage to Israel. Personal, communal, and cultural history cannot be ignored as our pilgrim speaks: "The seeds in our blood can't be dug out. They take root in the flow. . . ."

The book moves finally to the poems that explore being in midlife—for Baron that is marriage, children, and aging, dying parents. Searching for his religious roots and discovering new spiritual connections enables Baron to come to terms with human frailty and find ways to forgive, to accept, to see beauty in the imperfect. These are all aspects explored in his closing poems, from "Viduy...," "Of Elk and Marriage," and "Shabbat" to poems of hope and lightness in "The Park" and "Snools." As readers will see in a later book of Linfor's, although married life has its challenges, the light of love and fruit of children who bring delight and more light to their parents has a tempering effect on the darkness of the speakers' journeys. Readers sense hope and optimism. Finally, richness and complexity describe the narrative moments, the questions, and the understanding that happens in "What Now is Beauty?" and the final poem, "The Broom Tree." In the closing poem, a long narrative where the poet parallels his own journey with a sacred text of Elijah, the wanderer who found the Broom Tree, sat beneath it and pleaded with God to take his life, the reader senses that the poet and his speaker have finally arrived, faced down fear, and as the poet says in a stanza from his own story, "All at once, / I understand / with each day / I live less and less / for myself." With the interplay of the speaker's life details following each stanza of Elijah's story, readers will sense the timelessness within both men under trees, both breaking bread, both grounded in their physical being but also ready to give their lives for their God. For the poet, the journey from childhood to his travels to Israel to his marriage has led him to his home where he sits under the pomegranate tree. He says he knows why he was made to take his life's journey and in that faith, he proclaims, "I am ready. / I am afraid. / I am listening." *Under the Broom Tree* is an important first book for Baron. He is still young in his marriage and in raising his children. He has more of life's journey ahead of him, and readers trust that he will keep his ear close to the flow and keep moving.

~

As readers move from Baron's book into Eudy's *Bills of Lading*, Eudy offers some interesting insights into the placement of her book following Baron's: "My book is also a journey that grapples with a lot of spiritual questions. It's interesting because while Chris (Baron) grew up Jewish and has integrated Christianity into his identity as an adult, I grew up Catholic and have come to Judaism as an adult . . . we both still respect and connect with our religious histories, but we're finding our way in the context of a new set of religious and spiritual beliefs. . . ." Eudy explains the spiritual journey is central to her book; the readers will find poems as explorations and meditations of God and her relationship with God. Eudy credits many writers and thinkers such as Rainer Maria Rilke, Rumi, Mirabai, Paul Celan, Yehuda Amichai and others for their inspiration, particularly in exploring spirituality. She adds that she has turned to the pages of *The Song of Songs* as well as the ecstatic poetry in collections such as *Women in Praise of the Sacred*, edited by Jane Hirshfield.

Beyond the spiritual journey, readers will discover other journeys in the poems. Early on in a synopsis of the book, it's said that "her work, embedded in journey, reaches out and explores space, gender, and the life of the spirit." Before the opening poem of the book, Eudy offers a note to the reader, where she defines "bill of lading." She calls her poems "metaphoric receipts." Expanding on the metaphoric quality of the title words *Bills of Lading,* the poems can be seen as ". . . an attempt at understanding what it is to be human—our suffering, our family histories, our desire, our sex, our searching."

Attention to place and perception of what one encounters in urban or natural settings is important in Eudy's poems. She admits, "There is a love of motion, for being on the road, for wandering," but she also recognizes that many of the poems are grounded in place, inspired by her many travels across the country and abroad. As in "Denver Lull," the speaker never fails to note the little details in her surroundings. She says she has new eyes for Colorado and even when she has to catch the next bus after missing one, she celebrates the sunset and "red cherry billboards." In spite of struggles, the speaker has not shut off her connection to her world. Although a poem's tone may seem dark with bitterness and pain, Eudy's use of humor—whether ironic or wry—serves to lighten the tone. In the opening poem, "Bills of Lading," the speaker says, "I believe there exists a universal truth that when you want something, you will not get it." A reader might laugh with recognition here. Then a question is posed, "Or is it that it is no longer yours?" Within the prose poem, Eudy extends the question and possibility that it's "as though your fight for it withdrew it, released it for somebody else more qualified." So journey themes of the body and spirit balanced with poems in California settings, richness in words and phrasings, and variation in tone are qualities of Eudy's book.

As the reader moves further into *Bills of Lading,* complex tones are achieved in poems that are grounded in place such as "California Poppy" and "Persimmons." Readers will see a connection between the praise of the poppy and Linfor's "Matilija Poppy," for in both poems there is a sense of discovery and celebration for a quality in the flower that is often taken for granted or not recognized. While Linfor nurtures the upstart, almost weedy-stemmed, but fragrant and delicate bloom of the Matilija in her yard, Eudy stops her car and takes a close-up look—like she might with a close-up lens from her camera—and tells us, "having gone these ways / many times before unnoticing of the emerging / orange until, out of ordinary grass, I discovered a / poppy." The tone is wonderous and expansive as she writes, "As people, now utterly earth-bound, will probably always see the ocean of our history, I couldn't / help but believe the plant's body grew sea-green and budded anemones." She further describes with color language the poppy's appearance, its "neon blossoms" and the "sea spider inside," as she leads the reader to a question: "Out of ordinary grass, how can a thing be so bold as the fish that glows in the dark of the ocean floor?" In a third stanza she snaps a black and white photo and then must hop back in her car, leaving us with a tone of lament that as she drove away "the grass became ordinary again, and the roads became too windy for me to notice in / color radiant, temporary beauty."

As in some of Youmans' poems that include the scope of exploring seasons as well as singular fruit or tree as a device to explore a theme, in the poem "Persimmons," a poem written in unrhymed couplets, Eudy delivers a sometimes critical and other times redemptive look at the seasons, her hometown, and her own view of life. Eudy's speaker says she traces the seasons through an orchard. The redemption of the hometown and its questionable pursuits—delivered in list form ending in "methamphetamine"—is the grove line. The speaker moves to the fall season and tells us she is still grieving "love lost, I pay for a bucket / to fill with red-orange harvest. One after the other, I pluck / alone, under a sky of their ripe / heavy tart sweet. . . ."

In Youmans' "Of Light and Loss and Lemons" the speaker, too, grieves: "I mourn the loss of who I felt I could be with you." As Eudy's speaker tells us the solitariness of picking persimmons one by one, Youmans' speaker also admits, "Being alone in this pause / takes patience; a tree without blooms." Both poets revel in the sensation of the fruit, Eudy's persimmons "red-orange" and "heavy tart sweet—strange / to most Americans," and Youmans' lemons with their "yellow and white start / blossoms" and when cut in slices, "little rounds of cheer."

Eudy moves through the seasons in "Persimmons," and the tone shifts as the speaker tells us winter's spare gray reminds us that there will always be the dead and that spring can sometimes be annoying for "its refusal to stop coloring." The speaker tells us she resents spring's joy and "perkiness" and like a killjoy asks, "Where is the fruit in these?" when faced with the jade green leaves. The tone does not stay dark and pessimistic, though, for the speaker shifts and takes a closer look, as speakers often do in Eudy's poems. In beautifully simple, elegant language, the poet leads us to the "opening star of persimmon" deep in the green of the leaves.

Within place, the speakers in Eudy's poems struggle to come to terms with the human condition, the wanting and the rejecting. Eudy says, "I see the book as a grappling with some core struggles and connections in life, in relationships with others, be they human or not: with romantic partners, strangers, landscapes, the road, oppression, gender, and desire." Many of her poems explore desire, turn it over, and examine it from many angles. In attempting to make sense of desire, the speaker struggles to make peace with it, "hoping for some sort of release from it," Eudy explains, "and ultimately an acceptance of it being an integral part of being human." Influential writers who have encouraged her to be brave and take risks with themes of sexuality, relationships and oppression include Lucille Clifton, Louise Gluck, Marilyn Hacker, Nicole Brossard, and Fanny Howe.

The human condition is sometimes explored from a more general, distant view by a speaker who might be observing or interacting with strangers on a train or bus, or more intimately as between lovers who have just had sex or a person who has just had an awareness of herself as she travels alone. A series of poems follow each other in sequence and seem to move from a general witty critique to a biting observation and finally a detailing of a crisis moment on the road as we look at "The Boat Next to Illusion," "The Blue Line," and "Valley of the Shadow."

Warnings to avoid checking out the inside of the boat, stay away from night tours, and not talk to the captain are not elaborated upon but heap up as this poem, "The Boat Next to Illusion," descends into a witty end line stating, "Price: Negotiable." The speaker and the reader are amused but held at a distance from each other. In "The Blue Line," readers will see connections between Eudy's catalogue of strangers "riding the T" along a long list of stops, and Baron's poem "Absolution" with the speaker noting the flickering lights, the scratched Absolut Vodka sign, and the man down on one knee. Eudy plays with color and rhythm, moving back and forth between repeating short lines of "on the blue line" and longer lines depicting the sea of humanity in all of its conditions, "alone or coupled." Eudy says the poem "blends travel and the Boston subway with sadness, a social consciousness, and a tinge of hope."

It is important to note the nonlinear quality of the exploration and journey theme in Eudy's book. She writes in her note to the reader that many of the poems were written at different time periods around being employed as a driver. Chance encounters and unplanned happenings come up as subject matter just as they would on any road trip. Readers make a connection between Eudy's poems "The Blue Line" and "If I Didn't Have to Catch This Bus," for in both, the democratic spirit of traveling alongside strangers can be seen. The speaker ponders the "what ifs" and readers are reminded of Whitman's catalogue of hardworking, everyday Americans as he celebrated the open road. Readers are also reminded of the unemployed and the broken spirits. In portrait detail, a style that poet friends have attributed to her writing—language-based portraits, painted with words, sounds and concepts—she shows her recognition and acceptance of strangers she meets: "I would not have made the acquaintance / of the hairy-chested man on Valium / riding to Dayton, offering me / beef jerky and gum."

Then, in "Valley of the Shadow," Eudy delivers a driver in crisis, a speaker who has trucked down the dark two-lane roads of Appalachia, felt "delirious from not eating," closed in on and "lost in curves" and yet somehow passes through the crisis, by pulling over where light manages to pass through. The speaker seems to have suffered a panic attack, her body telling her things that perhaps her mind and spirit can't articulate yet. She says, "I lie in the thick dust and let the cool drift over me. / My skin for the first time feeling absolute shade."

Beyond the journey of exploring her connections and self through strangers she's met on the road or friends and lovers, Eudy's own spiritual journey is center to the inspiration for her book. Less narratively than Baron, but with story and images that can be metaphoric and resonate with outside texts or song, Eudy presents the reader with speakers struggling to come to grips with their spiritual journey and arrive at some acceptance of who they are in their beliefs. The longer, sectioned meditation form is seen in two important poems, "Imaging the Divine" and "Hymn of the Proselyte." In three sections, the poem "Imaging the Divine" reveals that the speaker's faith has collapsed, caved in, and dried up as we learn first that a perhaps mythical eunuch "collapsed inside me as memory of a once, a faraway love." As in Baron's "Making Aliyah" poem, it seems many wrong paths are followed and "the den caved in" for Eudy's speaker. Words like "burnt up" and "frizzled" describe the disaster. Hunger is acknowledged: ". . . there is / more hunger once the first hunger / is acknowledged." The speaker has awareness and feels guilt, but the books whisper otherwise. In the third and last stanza, the setting is a river where villages live. Eudy delivers a stunning mid-stanza line: "The time in which I've taken this body / is flat time—running long and drying up." The source for inspiration—whether communal or divine—is explored in poems that, perhaps because of the very subject, are often expressed in startling, memorable ways, such as the one just mentioned. Further, readers will find that many of Eudy's poems uncoil to powerful endings. At the closing of the poem, the speaker describes the mystery of how she has come to know and be able to write or tell a story. Although she has answered yes to a question of whether or not she could ever be self-defined, she counters, "But some / words were not handed to me because I asked / for them. Some memories, some rods / and hooks will pierce me, love, even as you / reach for me so tenderly now."

Another powerful poem that reveals the deep and complex struggle of coming to terms with one's faith is "Hymn of the Proselyte." It begins with a quote from *The Song of Songs*: "Then I went down to the walnut grove / to see the new green by the brook, / to see if the vine had budded, / if the pomegranate trees were in flower." The reader senses that the poem will be about a speaker who seeks, who looks for something alive—green by the brook, and beyond green desires budding and flowering—with maturing growth and nurturing. We read on into the opening three line stanzas of the poem and are given snapshots of scenes of clearly Catholic moments. Words and phrases tied to religion are spoken: "this is the word of the Lord," "Hail Mary . . ." and "Amen." We see a pious girl, an earnest lector, and a folk choir. In well-expressed words Eudy has her speaker suggest that "there is nothing / wrong with Jesus / but the God of childhood is inextricably tied / to parental / perspective / to what is human" and then perhaps closer to Eudy's own experience and in perfect-pitch sound and words that capture the image says, "and an emerging woman / will likely cut / her mainspring loose / under the weight / of scrutiny / or abuse."

A new stanza allows for a time shift and the speaker, now older, is returning to "a compassionate creator" and perhaps either once cast off or never really recognized.

The poet uses the image of a river opening again to the sea as a way to tell us the speaker has found her faith. In a shift to a new section of the meditation poem, the image of an uprooted western sycamore, one that came into being through fire blight's effects and now catches notice in the San Diego River serves as a metaphor for and echo of the opening quote of the poem and the tests the speaker has had to face in order to recognize how and where she is being called to faith in a God.

In the final section of the poem, the poet's speaker tells the reader that although she desires what she has found, the reader senses the complexity and struggle with her spiritual experience even still in her newfound faith in conflicting pairings of words such as "caress" and "stinger." The speaker asks us to look at her "bending at the knee . . ." and see the emerging yet not fully integrated spiritual woman who is "singing the Sh'ma / a Catholic girl / of an Apostles' / Creed. . . ." And in a last, memorable line, the speaker utters, "Can I help I like to pray." Eudy does not sacrifice her truth by tidying up the endings of her journeys or veiling the dilemma or struggle of change.

Within the poems in *Bills of Ladings*, Eudy offers many gifts. She is generous in her honesty and her openness to reveal the difficult times of being alone in relationships or alone in one's struggle with one's faith. Although the road feels dark at times in this book, readers know that we can trust this poet and be inspired to show the courage she does in speaking her truth. When we hear about truth, there can be lightness. With the many encounters between strangers, friends, lovers, family, and the divine in this book, in a poem "A Town in Massachusetts" placed near the book's end, it is heartening to hear the speaker's wish for others is pure and giving. Eudy fills the book with hope and "the hope for hope," as she says. "A Town in Massachusetts" is dedicated to friends. The reader senses that it is by communing in nature with those you can trust that a channel opens for stories to come to a speaker. Eudy writes, "Here we commune in a meekness / a sweetness that allows us / to open up notebooks . . . and to be judged only / by a creator so fine as to have made / these trees. . . ." And it is in this place that the speaker says she might wake up and have a story on her tongue. She says openly, "I might mimic your style and sing." Eudy speaks about the power of community in writing and how writers learn and borrow from each other, a realization all artists come to whether influences are contemporary or from the past. She tells her friends to look for themselves in her stories. Explorations of the power and gift of writing and storytelling come in other poems. A memorable line from "Boca del Cielo" reminds readers what the poet Eudy offers as a gift to her readers: "To write is to remember and to tell is to give."

Eudy's closing poem, "Blue Peter," resonates with the collection's metaphoric image of the lantern. The opening descriptive lines echo some of the language and events of poems throughout the book, for readers have heard in this book of sorrow, of faith being resurrected, and we've seen the color blue and the glow from light. The narrative moves in stichic form with internal rhythm and grace as it begins: "At the center of my sorrow / there resurrected a lighthouse. / A few creaky rooms spiraled / toward the lamp, / surrounded in the blues." The speaker climbs a lighthouse stairway. We are shown it is not an easy ascent by the speaker's posture, the tight grip and animal crouching. At the top of the climb, the journey up, there's discovery, and the speaker promises it will reveal her "faithful story." By the time we arrive at the closing of her book, we want Eudy as a friend, a sister traveler, perhaps a lover, and definitely a guide as illuminating as a lantern.

~

Poet Cali Linfor's *A Book of Ugly Things* follows as the third book in *Lantern Tree* and continues to shine a light into the darkness: as she says, "the poems examine things that cast the eye away." While it may be true that the poet has her reasons for exploring the "ugly things," it can also be said that for balance there is celebration, hope, joy, and discovery of beauty in this book. Linfor began writing poems about the unbeautiful a decade ago. "In this book, I think about the unbeautiful," she writes. "It is the base meditation. Everything is filtered through this lens."

Having been born with a genetic disability, Linfor feels that she has been freed from the standards of beauty, or as she says, "at least looks at them asymmetrically." In stating that she "wants to capture more complex mixed states of being and the process of coming to an acceptance of ugly things," she suggests that "these ugly beautiful things fall into a number of categories: male beauty, trauma, grief, illness, disability, apocalypse, spiritual dogmas, mythologies, failings of character, language, and nature—the domestic or man-made."

Linfor describes herself as a lyric poet and says, "Sound matters a great deal to me." Not only will readers discover that she is a formal poet who writes in meter and end rhyme, follows traditional forms of syllabics and varies stanzas from quatrains to triplets to the couplet, but she is also an experimental writer who plays with form and, for example, will include an exploded narrative alongside some narrative poems.

"Lyric in the Light" opens the book and within the formality of a syllabic form—the seven-syllable line—begins to examine the horrific effects of post-traumatic stress disorder (PTSD), one of the major explorations of the book, according to Linfor. Readers learn in both lyrical language and direct wording how the body reacts: "Burial of grief behind lung, / . . . . Mourning in both breath and blood." Then in another stanza, clear word choices detail the effects: ". . . the bowel contracts, panics, bolts." In the straightforward, clean language of these opening stanzas, readers will recognize poet writers like Raymond Carver who has influenced Linfor with his spare conversational language that can work in poetry, too. Other poets whose influence might be felt in this poem and others include Maxine Kumin for her story and compression of language, both qualities evident in Linfor's poem, as well as Lucille Clifton for her short lines and stark truth-telling. We are told for now that writing it down is not possible. However, the reader learns from this early poem that the poet knows how to begin the healing journey: "A naming ceremony, / for moments without sanction." Victims become "tongued again" with the "Word-Song."

The opening poem also introduces the act of hanging lamps in bare trees so that there can be brighter light. Linfor is aware of the darkness in poems and in some parts of the arc of the book that she explains includes the examination of "the plain, the overlooked, horrified and the rotting...captured and turned over in the hands." She says, "In a condensed number, those poems are hard to read," but she wants more for her readers and adds, "I want the readers to be able to take those ideas into themselves. . . ." She hopes for the intimacy that "really seeing something or someone brings—knowing and receiving the whole of a thing." A relationship can happen when the reader trusts the poet, continues on in the poem, on into the book, through and beyond the hard and ugly parts. So readers see the poet building signs of hope for healing at the end of the opening poem with the lantern and song. Some joy in imagery and word-song. There is the beginning of a trust and the promise of a relationship between the poet and readers.

Linfor states, "Balance in the book is vital to me." In "Matilija Poppy," she describes "a native showgirl" and convinces readers with her truthful statement that the woody eight-foot-tall plant is "ugly too / but so full of pollen and glitz, we don't see it." Readers will later see the connection to "Possession" where the speaker takes note of the bare nectarine beside the lovely fruiting winter orange tree and reminds us that though gray and stark now, it will bear fruit in the next season.

"Apocalypse" is a longer, sectioned poem that unfolds part narrative, and part exploded narrative with varying-length stanzas, rich in rhythm and image. Along with another poem in Linfor's book, "Stringfellow Acid Pits, Emergency Drills, and Smog Alerts," the subjects of fault lines, earthquakes, remembered childhood imaginings, and school emergency practices are detailed and investigated. In "Apocalypse" at the end of the first section, it is the children who know when something is wrong and not the truth. Classmates have practiced "duck and cover" and have sat still for a film in science class, but the poet gives them voice: "We know / this will not work." They see through the charade. And in another moment of the poem, the speaker admits, "I know I should not believe / the earth will remain generous, / food plentiful and the rain / sweet and drinkable." The poet details the trauma to other species and speculates that the earth may "shatter." This part of the poem resonates with other poems that examine trauma and its effects, beginning with the opening poem of the book. The reader learns to trust the young, the innocent, and the memories of the victims as they think back to what they witnessed in their youth.

The poem enlarges and within sections the poet examines icons from religion—masculine images of Jesus, Jesus on the cross. Then there's naming of food items rotated in the storehouse—a remembered tradition from another religion, a protection from wanting, from disaster. In a further section, the poet rounds out how a person's lifetime can be filled with visual images of disaster.

The adult speaker can now imagine the trauma, post-disaster. Besides the domestic worry of not enough food, not enough water, there is terror "trapped in the sinews / of our throats." The ecstatic and lyrical take over as "god" is addressed: "Oh, god, I believe / you are in every rock" and then "you are in me and outside / of me as your star falls / onto all of us / your other fallen stars." Knowing some of Linfor's influences as a poet can help readers appreciate the risks she takes, as in this longer poem. Beyond the influence of discipline and form, poet/professor Glover Davis taught Linfor and others: "Don't think you already know what the poem is about." He stressed being brave and walking through the door that a poem opens, and if we trace the arc of the poem from the opening moments of a childhood narrative to the adult speaker addressing her god, we can see Linfor's willingness to take risks and have patience in developing her images and concepts. "Apocalypse," for Linfor, is a centerpiece poem that she says she has been working on for ten years or so. She says, "I predate the current post-apocalyptic obsession with my own." Linfor would credit poets like Adrienne Rich for advising patience and James Dickey for technique in leaning into an idea for the long poem, in allowing obsessions, and nurturing the startling image—all elements of the richly crafted poem "Apocalypse."

From "Apocalypse" and "Stringfellow and Pits, Emergency Drills, and Smog Alerts," Linfor leads her readers deeper and more personally into her family history in "Ardith's Feast." As mentioned earlier, there is a link between Baron's poem about his Romanian grandmother who tells of his family's struggles to survive as she cooks latkes in her kitchen and Linfor's grandmother who, while kneading, flattening, and rolling out fry bread dough, explains her ways and instructs her granddaughter to eat the bread.

In the opening of the poem, the adult speaker becomes the young child again who startles at the sight of "only four fingers" as her grandmother mixes the dough. In italicized and indented stanzas, the speaker as child says, "I tug on your skirt" and then as adult implores to be told the story. The speaker wants details from this grandmother whom she shares a genetic disability with—how to have sex, how to nurse babies, how to be a woman. There is tension created between a granddaughter who implores her grandmother for more information and the grandmother who offers singular responses and who is perhaps more private and tight-lipped like others of the older generation. The grandmother tells the speaker that she covers her hand because she knows that "the sight of two shriveled fingers would frighten you" and in a seemingly more piqued tone says, "You want the whole story in the time it takes me to make bread." In a few broad strokes, Linfor gives the reader a very believable older woman who is a survivor, one who can be prickly and real, yet in the end no-nonsense and caring as she tells the granddaughter to "Eat the bread while it still shivers with the heat, love."

Following "Ardith's Feast," the poet leads us through a sequence of poems—"The Dark Question," "We Shoot Lame Horses," and "Adoration"— that continues to investigate disability and the questions it prompts as well as fears it causes for the family members and speaker. Although the journey through the poems is frank, dark, and painful, readers know that they can trust this poet because earlier she has shown us the power of love and care between family members who are survivors. We remember that she has demonstrated in earlier poems that scars can have a certain kind of beauty, that taking care of the dead is something she knows. In "In the Deep Line . . . ," the speaker tells us: she caught her dying mother's last, salty tear in her palm. In the sectioned poem "This Burning," she sits beside her dying grandmother and holds her grandfather's hand. The readers learn the strength of this no-nonsense, strong woman when Linfor writes, "I don't grieve the tending. . . ." She offers her truth: "I was loved so I loved."

Linfor's book accomplishes her desire to present the reader the reality of pain and non-standard beauty, side-by-side with courage and unconventional takes on beauty that inspire hope and courage. Whether the platform is family or nature, Linfor guides us through her investigation of what strikes us as ugly and hopeless to a new perception of life and bounty. In poems such as "Matilija Poppy," earlier connected to Eudy's "California Poppy" and also Eudy's "Persimmons" and Youmans' "Come Winter," readers see speakers investigating the perception of beauty and ugliness in plants, fruit trees, and seasons, letting those natural forces teach them lessons about life and hope. Linfor shows us in "Matilija Poppy" and in "Possession" that unconventional beauty can be found in a shrubby native plant and a barren nectarine beside a showy orange tree. She describes the nectarine's bark as scabby and the few leaves as "pointed fingers" that "startle," yet turns in the following stanza to the promise of fruit—life in the coming season. It is nature that teaches we humans, for Linfor's speaker is honest in her admission that upon first becoming caretaker to the trees, she didn't know what she was doing, and she hoped they weren't dependent on her for survival. She showed her trust in a force greater than herself, yet remained teachable by nature.

While giving us these lessons of hope and survival, we are struck by Linfor's many poems that speak of buried or unrecognized pain and terrifying fear. In poems such as "Wail," Linfor approaches the subject of fear and pain by remembering a childhood fear of a story she had heard growing up in her neighborhood about a wailing woman who in her grief would steal children. In poems such as "The Broom Tree" by Baron and others in the book, poets find their voices sometimes through sacred texts, myths, and cultural stories of their heritage. Further, once a poet establishes her voice, it can become clearer and stronger through her speaker, such as in Youmans' "A Conversation with Pain" and Baron's "Other Women and Oars."

In "Wail," Linfor describes the bodily effects of fear that lingers, reminiscent of the PTSD effects described in "Lyric in the Light," but this time more embellished, as in lines such as "our bellies float and twist / in a carnival of trembling." Still a stark line—"We bite down"—can quickly follow. The adult speaker admits she can carry the fear and pain around and not even know until it is touched. It is an old fear. The poem ends with a prose stanza that moves to the present with the speaker comforting her child who has awakened frightened from a bad dream. She talks to him and explains to him the why of bad dreams of monsters, something the readers can guess no one did for her as a child. Readers by now know that it is in Linfor's style to pursue one more thought and angle in this long meditative poem. The speaker tells us, "Children possess a sudden violence. The hard pinch of tiny fingers." She describes how a child can squish a bug and throw rocks to break things. She philosophizes that "A lack of malice makes it better but it hurts." And when she adds, "It all hurts," one cannot help but think that even the ones we love and trust the most—our partners, our children—still have the capacity to deliver "the hard pinch" and surprise us once more with pain and fear.

Linfor has told us that her hope for the book is that it offers intimacy to the reader, part of the balance to the exploration of dark themes, and by this point in the book, the reader can trust that this poet and her speakers know how to be human, know how to live as a human who tends to the dead, as well as one who attends a birthing—witness to what makes us human beyond flesh, blood, and bone. We hear that cry of a newborn, her first song. For Linfor, intimacy is "pleasurable and uncomfortable. . . ." In her closing poem, "Ugly Things," she opens playfully and with some humor as she admits to reading the end of a book first and then turns to the reader with the same question. Soon, though, she draws readers into her personal life. Perhaps even she has had to learn to trust us, her readers, just as she has hoped for our trust. At last, she is in the present, and she brings her dearest ones into her poem—her four-year-old son, her husband. And from that moment on we are in the "pleasurable and uncomfortable," for we learn of her conversations with her son, his unique and yet so recognizable childlike view of the world. He has told her "he only likes ugly things. Sharp teeth, / the color black, dirt, scabs, exhaust / from trucks, he collects them."

We are in the midst of a conversation between our poet and her son. The poet's instinct to include us, let us hear her response, is so smart and vital to our growing closer to her. She tells him "all of these things / can be quite pretty as well."

His response is true: "He growls." Knowing her own child intimately, she interprets and tells us, "He does not like it / when two things are true at once." And then we are in the car where the son charms his mom, in the way parents know their children can, with his growing list of ugly things—dog drool, scribbles, a sinkhole—and next at dinner when mom has her son tell dad more of his list—lint, snake hole—and dad is laughing, and finally in bed. The poet takes us along with her and we are the fourth in the family—seeing and hearing, giggling and hopeful. The poem does not stop here, though.

The final effect of the book is crucial for Linfor. She says, "It is important to me that the book not be triumphant. I think that is a false extreme that cannot be maintained." So in the last stanzas, the poet shares that she knows well that her son will be exposed to horror one day. She deflates us with the reality of the inevitable. Still she adds some balance by promising that there will be comfort and declares, "We are ready. / We have practiced." Linfor has delivered on her promise at the end of her book not to "overcome" but also achieves her wish to show readers it is possible "to live in fullness."

Sabrina Youmans' book *Pacific Standard Time* begins with an introductory quote of the German poet Rainer Maria Rilke that resonates not only with the important themes of her book but possibly also with many of the explorations of the other poets in *Lantern Tree*. Rilke speaks of attaching oneself somewhere in nature where there is strength and abundant readiness. Readers have heard about being ready in Linfor's closing poem. Rilke advises moving forward, reaching out with joy. Readers have witnessed speakers in the other poems who have with humor and celebration of others—even strangers along the journey—found joy and love. The four poets are each striving to live in the present moment, have hope in today and the future, and find a way to transcend their pasts—whether by acceptance of what was—to be just that—or through transformation of past traumas to more enlightened perspectives. More than any connection to the other poets' themes, perhaps Youmans begins with Rilke's quote because it touches on several themes and concepts she explores in her book: the theme of loss and learning to adapt; taking joy and comfort in nature; discovering the transformative power of moving forward toward distances. Rilke speaks of the effort to "to dissolve the foreign body of pain . . ." in exploration and transformation, thereby allowing for the possibility of a gap or space left in its place, the concept of lacuna that Youmans introduces the reader to in her opening poem.

Although "Lacuna" opens in narrative detail about Youmans' family history, she quickly explodes the narrative form and introduces striking images with fresh and vibrant language that as she has said she hopes "leaves room for readers to create connections and meaning without losing contact with the poem." After the poet sets down the narrative details of her parents' fight on the patio, she moves away for a general assessment that "they search / for something in each other / to only find it missing." Then Youmans delivers a stunning line—breaking apart the narrative further—that not only exemplifies the meaning of the word lacuna but is emblematic in form as it stands alone with space above and below it. She writes, "Even bone has open spaces." Here the use of what artists call white space or negative space is as powerful as the words themselves. Youmans cites language poets such as Rae Armantrout as a major influence, as well as other poets such as T.S. Eliot, Emily Dickinson, and Robert Frost. Armantrout wrote a memoir, *True,* in which in retelling her upbringing and family history, she tries to investigate what is true and let stand the gaps in her relatives' stories about events and each other.

Beyond introducing the concept lacuna and its potentially transformative power of gaps and space, Youmans begins her exploration of loss. We see snapshots of how loss affected her father. Her deftness with language serves her as she declares, "We can never hear loss." "We can never fill our loss."

And then there are the images that enrich and become emblematic, fruit and the idea of transformation: "I was fruit and now I am flower."

Youmans describes her form preferences as mostly free verse with couplet and triplet formations to provide structure. She also plays with syllabics. Although Youmans may have more formal structures as mentioned in some of her poems, she admits she loves long lines and long exploration poems. In comparing their poem subjects and style, Eudy says that both love to play with language and contemplate the nature of life, but Eudy recognizes, too, Youmans' more overflowing and ecstatic writing. In discussing her meditative nature, Youmans writes, "My process is to write on one indelible image or event and see where it takes me." She strives to "create a layering of images and an ethereal, introspective tone." Meditative section poems follow in the first part of the book, introducing us to the landscape of Southern California and the idea of finding rest, beauty, and joy in nature, and the now is reinforced in poems such as "Union Station," "Four Graces," and "Abundance."

Pairing "Gravity" and then "The Tribe Ignites" back to back provides readers with the power of Youmans' vision. She recognizes that our experiences can leave us wanting, our needs not met, and she can state that directly and without sentiment, as she does at the end of "Gravity": "Chasing butterflies, / our wanting / may be expected / but impossible to obtain. / We may never have everything we need." However, Youmans does not leave the reader long with this realistic, if not dark, place. She builds hope and courage in her reader as she introduces the image of the lantern tree and the vehicle of finding a guide to lead the way. She implores, "Let us experience / Her clean heat / of the unbearable." From guide to lit lantern on the tree, the poet hopes the reader will take in the image and be transformed, gain courage and acceptance of life on life's terms. Youmans and Linfor become kindred souls in understanding and acceptance of life, in Linfor's words as "more complex mixed states of being" and that "two things are true at once." Nearing the end of Youmans' "The Tribe Ignites," readers are encouraged to "shine the light on / each awful moment / as proof of existence— / place the dreamy and the unbearable / side by side under the same lamp."

The middle section of Youmans' book, "California Incline," traces the arc of relationships and cycles to the upheaval of change and transformation. In "We Build," within the framework of lovers in an intimate moment, Youmans constructs from language and imagery borrowed from the building trades the relationship of these two people. She opens, "[P]ress our bodies, / our lives together / and a city grows / from our tangled forms." Readers experience her vivid imagination, "I settle you; pull you closer, / conveyer belts and elevators rise, / in tones of grays, sepias, putty and buff." The concept of lacuna enters the poem in lines like ". . . here in the freshly sawed naked wood / of a new door at our threshold / opening to space and more space; / we pause before entering." The presence of space—lacuna—and the act of pausing are vital signs of change and growth. The poem doesn't promise that the relationship will end in trust and permanence, but there is learning.

Through interactions in the natural world—the cycles of seasons, the stages of seed to bloom to fruit, and the stillness of a bird on a shoreline—the poet shows us we can and must move forward, begin to trust. In "Come Again, Winter," the poet offers a graceful acceptance of fall releasing into winter. Through the softness of sounds and tones in word choices such as "ushers," "hushed" and "fluttering / ease" to painterly images like "rain of papery gold," "tree feathers," and "saffron flowers," the reader is coaxed into joining the poet in her invitation to winter to "Come again . . . / we shed for you. / Let us make room / for your clean cruelty." And finally at the end the poet announces, "we are change / and we are ready."

It is as if from the stripped-down state of winter and its clean cruelty that speakers in the poems that follow "Come Again, Winter" are able to look at their own life choices, men, and female identity in a clearer, more realistic way. In "Between States" the speaker admits, "I've spent years / between locations / waiting for forces to propel me / into another state / or take me back." The tone is fatigue. In "Lunar House" the speaker proclaims, "I will try to see men as they are, not as I want them, / and to choose wisely." In a sectioned poem, "Bodies of Water," with Youmans' powerful command of language and images of water, the speaker does the hard work of seeing things as they are and not as she wants them to be and is then able to begin her transformation. The speaker says, ". . . I realize we do this with each other / pretend we are someone else together— / we try to make it work but neither of us is ever happy." Then the poet transforms that statement into an image of "silver, slippery liquid / holding no shape or meaning / other than necessary." The poem becomes an "exploration of identity, pretending to be something and transforming into a strong woman," says Youmans.

In beginning the last section of her book, Youmans faces pain—in its multidimensional form—head on. She has been preparing herself and her reader in the sections leading to "How to Explain Loss." In the long, sectioned poem titled "A Conversation with Pain," the speaker lets pain know exactly where the two of them stand—no mincing around with declarations like "I do not want you. / I know you too well. / You frighten me." She has let pain have it right between the eyes, stating her fear and pausing to breathe in and breathe out, using imagery of daisies and thistles. She keeps moving forward with her truth and clear vision. She states that a man in her life has been "an unreliable narrator" and then we see what she has had to endure. She begins a short litany of men and some complaints against them, grounded by their deeds and conversation. The poem's form and detail fascinate and inspire the reader. Youmans' maturity and courage are evident as she soon turns the focus of the speaker on herself, admitting, "Some people do not like me. / I am interesting, if sometimes beautiful. / An avocado, a kiwi, not necessarily a peach." The short, terse nature of the line structure works with the straightforward, truth-telling of the speaker. The imagery of fruit reinforces the speaker's sense of her identity. The speaker works through her pain and loss. She owns it.

An important poem, "Out of the Blue," demonstrates how Youmans balances the investigation of the personal in her exploration of pain and loss by presenting other poetic approaches to how humans learn to see things as they are, to recognize that loss cannot always be reconciled. Youmans describes "Out of the Blue" as an "epic tale of a tragic love story . . . with lightning woven throughout . . . a close look at science and how to face the unbearable and survive." Drawing on readings about the nature of how lightning works and also two accounts of people struck dead by lightning, Youmans builds a narrative that sometimes explodes with imagery, action, and realizations. These moments of clarity strike, almost unexpectedly for the reader, in the midst of the chaos and sometimes just before, as in the line "the current will flow through you, pass through your body, change you." Another ironic line comes after someone is killed, "The natural world offers relief until it strikes you down." A survivor who witnessed a friend struck down tells others, "I cannot accept that it happened for a reason, nor can I really accept that there is no reason."

For some survivors, the way to adapt and move forward comes from the voice of a healer, a guide. We go back to the lantern tree. The survivor is told she must go back into the night and "face what cannot be faced—the loss. . . ."

Near the end of the book's final section, out from the dark and truth-telling moments of those poems, readers emerge with the poet and her speakers to new growth, ". . . surviving green calls out for more light, more oxygen, more life" ("Tecolote Winter Walk"); to the wish for one's ". . . own space, in water . . . ," "moving with the currents," yet "holding place in the current," ("For My Sister"); to the whispering welcomings of cumulus clouds, "There is no distinction between us, waves and ocean. / We are too close to exist on our own"—a line that speaks as a connection to Baron's idea in "Absolution" that "We are closer than stars, / billions of times closer than we are far apart."

The poet has shown us facets of loss—familial loss, adult love loss, unexplainable loss, and self-inflicted loss. We have seen how some learn to recognize that loss cannot be reconciled. Loss causes deep pain and needs space and gaps to be recognized, examined, and then inhaled and breathed out. Above all, loss has been shown to lead to change and transformation.

In "For My Sister," the poet circles back to the family narrative that opened her book. And now the speaker's tones and words take on a sense of connection and acceptance when she says, "I am no better or different from our parents. / Built from their breath and touch / they live here in me and I live between them." The very images of clouds in "Of Heaven and Earth" are emblematic of the "ephemeral." We are told ". . . the shapes continue to change, / they allude to disappearance, / instability and being left unfulfilled. / 'Let it go,' they sing in chorus." And again, another poet's words confirm the wisdom of the chorus and suggest the eternal when Baron's speaker in "Absolution" says, "I follow the steam up and up / where it circles against a dark sky / and for a moment breaks the clouds / where starlight pours / into stillness . . ." and we are told that the silence "veils" a people who have struggled for visibility but will continue to breathe and survive in the "sovereign / glory of life / worth living."

By the end of the last poem of her book, "Of Heaven and Earth," Youmans has found her own "personal language to express what seems to elude understanding"—something she says she has wished and worked hard for—when she brings the reader back to the image of the lantern and the power of language that can articulate how "Light catches these droplets / and changes them into / glowing lanterns. / The answers / adorn eyelashes / in dew— / blessings / for transformations."

~

In closing this introduction to *Lantern Tree: Four Books of Poems*, it is important to mention something of the process of the poets coming together to bring us their book and also their history, working together in the writing community of San Diego. Linfor offers a thought that she says still holds true from the poets' earliest proposal: "Our poems are a way to find equilibrium—to hold a shape." She also adds that in being responsible to each other, "we knew that with such continual reading of each other's works that connections between the books would organically arise. Each book would be vitally influenced by the others and become a whole book together. We trusted that process and in each other. . . ." Through the process of working through their books together, Baron describes a very deep connectedness between the poets as well as in their books. He says, "We are so different, yet our desire for truth, and love and acceptance, seems to resonate so much in our poems. All of us love adventure, that's for sure."

In the spirit of adventure, the poets established the Mayday Poetry Workgroup back in February of 2010. Linfor founded and organized the group, wanting more than poets who would just critique each other's works. She envisioned they would "come together to be poets . . . create a space where when we crossed the threshold . . . this part of ourselves would come to the fore, so to speak. We don't really talk about our work life, just poetry and our very personal lives." The group meets monthly and has a cyberspace home as well. Linfor explains, "Being a poet means writing poems, of course, but it is more than that. We work to support each other in our individual visions of what it means to be a poet. We work at being poets. We labor together. This laboring is the mission of the workgroup and out of this commitment each poet sets his or her own goals and uses the group to reinforce those decisions."

Readers can learn more about the four poets in the biography section of the book. They will tell you about their own academic backgrounds and writing training—these poets' lives intersected in time and place as each were mentored by poet professors and each other in the MFA Program at San Diego State University—as well as their influences far and wide from noted poets and from other outside passions and fields.

Lastly, think of these four poets as lanterns—each glowing, sometimes flickering, faltering, almost sputtering to an end, but then sparking back, burning brightly and lighting our way. If any of us have stopped reading poetry, these poems will remind us of just how good a poem can be—the experience of being transported by an image, a sound, language that breathes, a story. If one of us has never read poetry, let this be the invitation, the introduction. If we have always loved poetry, let us accept this offering from these gifted poets. Let us interact.

These four poets stand ready, open, and vulnerable. Ready to share some of what's brought them to their commitment on the page, in their throats, releasing words—their messages—to the air, to us. We readers will hear their coaxing and witness the effort of the poets and speakers. Baron speaks for all of us when he expresses the complexity of true being: "I am ready. / I am afraid. / I am listening."

Nancy Cary
San Diego 2012

Under the Broom Tree

Chris Baron

For Ella, Asa, and Samaria. And for Caylao: little girl, you are a bundled lantern I drape on the tree of my heart, bright in the wilderness.

“Not all who wander are lost.”
—J.R.R. Tolkien, *The Lord of the Rings*

“Then, at one particular corner of the gooseberry patch, the change came.”
—C.S. Lewis, *That Hideous Strength*

“Send forth your light and your truth,
let them guide me, let them bring me to your
holy mountain to the place where you dwell.”
—*Psalm 43:3*

Contents

THE LANGUAGE OF RIVERS

no doubt you walk
where I walk

feel mud of this fading river
soft and cold through your boots

on mornings like glass
along the river that calls its own name

I watch it every time
it overflows its banks

seeps into dry fields
soft pressure uproots the rooted

done

undone

you race water
your feet slip and shake
covered in mud half-stuck in water falling

all over yourself
legs weak from the fear that you might be the only one
who heard the river say anything

do you remember what it said?
did it have a voice?

is this ancient water?
does it see when you first came to its banks
broken and quiet your hands over your knees
head buried?

yes

does this water listen?

hasn't it every time?

yes

you are shocked to know that the water will even waste its time with you
when you allow yourself to listen

how long until you put your ear to the flow
allow yourself a chance to believe

so here you are
sometimes sitting in your car
listening to the radio
the DJ is telling you how to feel

your sister tells you that you've snapped
you haven't paid bills in months
since the river first told you to come every day
since you first heard its sweet hum of consistency

you step out of your car
pull a sandwich from your small brown bag
pull off the crusts feed silvery fish swimming

in all the books you've read rivers don't talk
it's usually the trees that tell the stories

what do you hear when you let yourself drop
your unprotected ear to that stream
that music of questions or answers of what it might be like
to find your own source
to flow into a widening mouth of salt and blue

no stagnant pools just the cold and constant push of every moment
    what do you find when you dunk your head into that sudden water?
        what is this unexpected change where your eyes and ears and nose fill up

    and you find yourself spitting in the grass
    your head in an upside down pounding?
        these are your first words

this river is the heart where you are
    this river
        a quiet flood

HIDING FROM DUCHAMP

Descent
I walk the studio at night, the redolence
of oil, chemicals settle on my tongue.
The brushes harden on dried palettes.
A quiet swelling surrounds me
of unborn figures, the indistinguishable
blues and greens, rough etchings,
images depicting successive movements of a single body.
Most formless, but some with painted on eyes
that follow me to the core of the studio
where the tight stretch of empty canvas holds
itself in the cradle of an easel.

Exploration
The paint tubes unopened lie on the floor
almost ready to burst.
Unskilled, I mix them, combining color
with newspaper print and foil.
All night I cover the canvasses
with misshapen nudes taking walks
down staircases lined with hand-painted silk,
until my shirt, glazed in wet acrylic, reflects
the sun through tiny ceiling windows.
I slip away to bed as if I had never left,
the overcolored sheets twisted to a rainbow.

Futurism
The Artist returns, breaks glass,
moistens clay, stirs fiberglass.
She begins with graphite and oil
on canvas, vows, like Duchamp, to never repeat herself,
doesn't paint over the crude etchings of her son.
Instead she builds on them, combining acrylic
with resin. She mixes all these things, the glass,
the clay, the brush itself. Each image separate,

each figure suspended in time and space.
Features once flat rise from the canvas,
rough as epoxy, singular as fingerprints.

ORIGINS

Grandma sat us down at the long pine table,
fed us spoonfuls of apple butter on dry white toast,
the peppered latkes frying on the stove.
With our feet dangling from the bench,
she told us stories about her parents,
in the hills, on the farm, before America.
I asked her if we were American,
told her about the Black girl in my class
who shook her head and said she was African,
even though she had never been there.
Grandma held us both by our cheeks
and whispered, "We are all Americans now."
I smiled, asked her if I should tell my teacher
I was Romanian, even though I had never been.
She put a hand on her back,
bent over and swung her arm
up and down, until the spatula
scratched the ceiling and scuffed the floor.
"This is how we did it! Cutting, stacking
until the wheat was piled so high
we almost drowned."

She put a plate piled with latkes
on the center of the table
and poured us each a gingerale.
"Tell them!" she said. "Tell them all."

FIELD TRIP

After school, before cartoons,
I crack the studio door,
stunned by a wave of Mozart,
toxic smells of oils and cigarette
smoke. Women, naked, pose
on velvet sofas, between
palm trees, straddle sawhorses.
They don't notice me.
I've seen them before.
My mother, in its center,
spins like a whirlwind, consumes
everything with brush strokes.
I ask her to sign my
permission slip for the park,
the simple morning walk
from P.S. 6, where
we'll gather near the statue
of Hans Christian Andersen,
and listen to stories
just as she once did.
Somewhere between pain and delight
        her eyes twitch with memory
when I ask her again, twice,
and on the second, she twists
without a look and splashes
        the white page,
                with red.

STILL LIFE

The model's nude frame
exhausted against
a tall, peacock chair,
her long hair
threaded through
wicker lace.
So enmeshed in canvas,
the Artist doesn't look,
instead improvises
brush strokes,
re-invents the nude's form,
creates still life,
disappears for the day.
The nude watches
me as I watch her:
the thinness of eyes,
puffiness of lips,
hands on hands
with long reaching fingers
painted and slick.
Hands that walk along
her body when
suddenly she finds
that she is alone,
and I am curious.
        It wasn't the first time
she shaped her hand like a C
and fit it into my crotch,
my legs
buckling from her
soft pressure.
Eyes sealed and wet,
mouth
too dry
to scream,

limbs numbed to confusion,
long before I knew
she was beautiful.

FIRST KISS

Fat kids don't have girlfriends.
Friends yes, but not kissing,
not even in third grade.
So imagine my surprise
when once, in the backseat
of our '77 Caddy,
on the drive home
from the birthday party,
Tonya, her quiet eyes in mine,
put her braid on my shoulder,
and kissed me, twice.
The first kiss struck my nose,
then squarely she found my lips.
The next day, at school,
I spent hours staring
out the window, my shoulder
bending in memory of the braid.
My fingers pushed against my mouth
trying to remember the cold
suddenness of her lips and breath
that made me.

CENTRAL PARK ZOO

> *If you can't understand what's keeping you in, the will to get out soon becomes confused and ineffectual.*
> —Daniel Quinn

At the Central Park Zoo
I once held the hand
of a baby gorilla.
I remember the delight,
the wonders of the world
uniting under an autumn sun.
Her thumb, slightly scaled and black,
curled around my hand
in friendship.

Later, after the keeper
took away the infant,
my mother whispered to me,
for the first time of a thousand to follow,
the story of the elephant who
ate her library book when she was a girl.
My father remained distant,
smoking on a bench,
already looking past his
seven-year-old boy.

It would not be long until
I began to see in a different way—
the lion in a desperate pacing along hay and brick,
and seals swimming endlessly from shore to shore.
I found that the gorilla house was only a box
of metal where the silverback rested his head on the cold bars
looking out toward the light and air
unable to comprehend his own question.
I too began to look for a way out.

MY CIVILIZATION CASE

Only the rocks live forever.
—Gray Wolf, *Centennial,* James Michener

Three of us pile in the GMC,
pull dust clouds to the base of Arizona's Four Peaks.
Rodriguez' map reads, "Indian Ruins."
I collect rocks down the first deer trail I find,
turn stone from stone: topaz, quartz, jade,
the ruins scattered to invisibility.
A fire pit steams in the center of Rodriquez' X
like an old calendar, but that is it.
The world takes time to reclaim itself,
even takes back its rocks.
No cave walls describe the hunt, or stars
exploding in the heavens. No hand print
signature in soft clay, or etched sandstone,
or vision of the Crab Nebula,
the symbol that unified civilizations
across an Earth still distant.
No sundial, no first construction of time,
there's no presence here of life before us.
Until later, when I empty my pockets
on my desk, rocks collected.
Each stone chipped at its edges,
sharpened. Each one an arrowhead,
a carving tool, a stone knife,
pieces of something. Nothing.
I seal them in my "Civilization Case,"
knowing I'll find nothing more
or less valuable than jade, sandstone, or shale.

DOG HILL

I bend on the street corner, relieved.
The melody of prayers
spilling from my lips,
locked in practiced repetition.
    am I a man?
The city's lost inside me,
the bridges, Yankee Stadium.
I see the good in rain,
the truth in my father
like the uncertainty
of the first snow.
    am I a man?
The edge of Dog Hill marks winter,
snow lines hide the drop of the hill,
a speedway of racing toboggans.
I pull my own Golden Eagle
to the edge of the line, push off,
freefall in biting wind.
    am I a man?
At the 96th street playground,
our eyes wide at the intricacies
of the metal slide complex,
impossible stairs entangled
in stairs, a cage in the center,
the mouth of the slide
unreachable, and inside,
Rebecca Mendel,
brown hair pulled tightly
in a ponytail—the thought
of her hair let down
had brought me here.
    am I a man?
At the museum, my father
shows me our heritage.
Things never permitted,

once invisible, are now alive.
He shows me, "Holocaust,"
fills in maps empty until now.
The photographs are pale black and white—
families gather, light candles,
hold each other, walk together,
load on trucks, trains, wagons,
children smile. Why wouldn't they?
This could be their greatest adventure.
They gather at a street corner,
like tiny, full-grown men.
    am I a man?
My father cups his hands around my face,
whispers, "Never again." And I see for the first time
the fragile beauty of words,
of cities beneath cities, morning snow,
and returning home.

THE GREEN BOX

When you left the first time,
we had seventeen dollars,
an empty apartment
and no way out but ourselves.

I rode my bicycle
along the Marina Green,
canceled guitar lessons,
readied myself for a storm.

I sold my comics for half
their value, gave the money
to her. You never knew.
Months later, they pulled me

from math class. Other kids,
jealous, watched me walk
from the middle of algebra to the office.
You called to tell me you were fine.

Promises are impossible for you.

You filled a box with money,
stuffed it full. The box, green,
shipped that morning, on its way.
I told her about the box

while she breaded the chicken,
you know the kind I love—
small pieces, boneless,
garlic salt, crispy on the edge.

She didn't hear me.
The first welfare check bought us
twelve dollars in groceries,
her cigarettes, paid our rent.

She gave me five for school.
I checked the mail every day.
New cities took care of us.
We always survived on her talent.

Soon there was a house,
threaded together with food, pictures,
television, twenty dollars a week
for me. I wondered how the green box

would find us when we moved.
In the coldest nights, when our roof
was held in thick snow,
I would climb down from the loft,

turn the burning embers, add wood to the fire,
warm myself. I heard her screaming for you,
thumping her shoulders against thin walls,

her screams echoing, freezing me alone,
and that was the closest I could ever come to you.

SUMMER

for the girl

The two of us
climbed barefoot
up the trunk of the deep-rooted oak,
the branches a ladder, so high up.
We reached for the rope,
felt the water stir beneath us.
I waited while you always went first.
I understand now the grace
of your red and white sundress,
brown hair tied up into pigtails,
the edges turned blonde from the sun.
You were never scared to jump.
You swung and kicked yourself
as far as you could,
scratching your legs on branches,
holding on so tight your fingers burned.
I watched you disappear into water
and I never felt safe, or ready
until I looked down,
saw you floating backwards,
calling me, splashing, laughing,
and when you had smiled long enough,
I too grabbed the rope,
waited for you to call me.
My toes curled on the edge,
waiting to jump.
Sometimes now,
when I am on the edge
of things,
I hear your voice,
smooth as river-rock,
gentle as water-glass,
the August wind.

WAKING THE BOATS

In the quiet of early morning,
we sleepwalk through
boathouse doors,
loosening our long limbs,
stretching sinewy muscle
tightened from the practice that never ends,
the row, the lift, the run.
The heat of the stretch spreads,
our faces grow clear,
scratchy voices smooth,
echoing through the boathouse,
awakening the boats.
We shift them on their racks,
rig the seats with fresh oil,
bitter-smelling and slick.
I unhitch the door to the bay,
watch it slowly lift.
Our reflections stare
in the silent water,
in the dry, whiteness of morning.
Lowering the boats gently,
fashioning the oars to the oarlocks,
we climb into the shell,
so near the water
our reflections disappear.

OTHER WOMEN AND OARS

This isn't my life. Nothing here is mine.

You stand outside, swing the hose in the dark,
cover yourself in water, pretending rain.

You've changed your rituals again. You no longer speak
from the places I understand.

I buy cartons of lemonade, the kind you like,
sugar water that makes your throat ache.

You're looking at me, and maybe this time disagreeing.
You are pulling my shirt off, remembering.

Your frustrations are suddenly about the color of bed sheets.
You wrap them around you—stop eating breakfast.

And we finally talk. That's when I like it best, you about the long nights,
the moon too bright keeping you awake.

I explain the length of oars, the need for ultimate balance, "the boat
is no wider than my shoulders." You laugh at how phallic it all is.

The house offered you nothing, the murderous structure of wood.
You asked for the flow of water, and I promised it.

I know water, the comfort of a body almost weightless, the impossibility
of control, the power of bodies that skim its surfaces.

The streets fill up with water, racing down gutters, holding up traffic,
blocking escape. Puddles grow inlets.

I wake early for practice. The anticipation of the long row
won't let me sleep. I smell like you.

I explain how the harder you pull, the more tension you make in water.
This creates a puddle—the larger the puddle the faster you move.

Your face burns in the cold clear sweat of waiting. There is no joy in what
you know will not come, a question, an answer. We have fallen away.

My muscles ached before the row. I felt the oar's bend,
the indication of strength, the crush on the water, the lifting boat.

You stayed in the house alone not because you didn't want to see me,
not because you didn't want my skin next to yours.

The lifting boat, the crush of water, once eight now one, the boat lifting,
the glide on the water, the drag disappears, flight.

The rain soaks our bed. The damp indentation of a curled body
wrinkles the sheets. You've left again, and I don't doubt my confidence.

I rest in your choice.

I've moved the bed under the window again, cleaned the desk, won the
Head of The Charles, learned to boil rice.

I have separated myself from you and others. My hands are again my own.

ABSOLUTION

The Culver Line
I grab the F train on 82nd Street
to make the journey to my Aunt Cookie's house,
the neighborhood where the women burn on
the sidewalk lawn-chairs.

15th Street Prospect Park
In the tunnel I look for a seat,
but there are none because the grandmothers',
hands clutched on purses, will never get up.
They are fastened to a life they did not choose.

The ceiling lights flash inside plastic banners.
On one, inside a scratched-off portrait of Absolut Vodka
are the words,
"rescue me."

Church Avenue
Out of the tunnel, light is sudden and dull,
pressed against curved windows and automatic doors,
an untamed dimness, warm breath against glass,
not figures dancing, but slow and deliberate in its precision.

Ditmas
My watch is broken, and I stay standing
while my legs ache waiting for Avenue P and Quentin.
I search for the familiar—Misha's Deli,
children on metal roller-skates, stickball
down the center of Rugby Road all the way to Flatbush.

In the train, the words "rescue me" begin to flicker on and off.
Suddenly, I feel the weight of my own decisions. They push down,
giant, awkward hands along my shoulders,
a heaviness of mistakes and time spent.

Bay Parkway
The subway misses its stop racing the Culver line.
There is a man breaking down along metallic rivets of the train car floor.
He is on one knee now; quavering, his face is pushed into his hands.
I can't tell if he is laughing or crying or praying. He is squeezed into himself.

Rescue me. The words stand at the door of the train,
they reflect back at me in the doors of the car opening and closing.
On the other side of the doors, I see myself walking, holding a briefcase
overstuffed with scraps of paper flying from its mouth.

They float to the ground, tiny butterfly wings
unfolding and readable.
The key I promised Mrs. Goldberg in third grade that I would never lose;
scribbled-over hearts of girls, a valentine from Rebecca Mendel
in the shape of a lion that read, "My heart roars for you."
Live in the woods with the bears.
Hunt goblins.
Be a fireman.
A bronco with a gun rack.
A map leading north.
Marry Sophia Lauren or Raquel Welch?
Jennifer Connelly when she was in *Labyrinth*.
The name of another girl in unreadable ink.

Kings Highway
Rescue me,
because here I am now alone.
The train moves at light speed, but I stand.
I am waiting to get to where it isn't dark.
A light in a dark place cannot comfort itself—it needs other lights,
like galaxies in the crowded universe—
beautiful vortexes spinning uncontrollably,
and they don't let up until they are full of stars packed with the power
of creation and destruction and creation again,
but they too are alone, all alone, billions of times further away
than they are close to one another.

We are galaxies filled with swirling light and luminous bodies.
We attract other bodies into our orbit as we move.

We are closer than stars, billions of times closer than we are far apart.
Rescue me. I am closer now than ever before.

Avenue P

The light pouring in
through the metal framed windows
opens my eyes.
The words
wretch from my own mouth.
The train car is full,
awake, a chorus now
over a Brooklyn skyline.
The light is pouring in.
It's pouring
so brightly
I close my eyes,
and I ask one last time
before the doors open,
before I reach my stop,
before I step back into the sunlight,
before I live one more second of my life,
rescue me.

LIFE UNWORTHY OF LIVING

Lebensunwertes Leben

I am quiet
in my own history.
I walk a smooth stone
between my fingers,
along my hand,
in utter silence
writing poems
about the Holocaust.
It's been six decades;
I wasn't even there, yet
my mind won't let me believe
what my heart is living through.
The memories rise
in the voice of my grandfather,
so I go there again, and this time
with my own children.
This time not alone.

I'm on my knees holding them.
They are staring at me.
We are outside. It is cold,
and our coats are torn.
There is a man in a dark hat,
his eyes are made of wood,
his hands are clothespins.
He hangs us on his line one by one,
tells us that we are . . .
"life unworthy for living."
I pull them close to me,
whisper in soft ears
at that same moment
not to be afraid.
"G-d will look after you."
In the absolute silence,

I can only hear
the scrape of the train
coming in over the voice
of the clothespin man,
the iron wheels grinding,
and the shrieks of the train whistle,
so loud that it is utterly silent.
Yet even in a memory
which is not my own,
I follow the steam up and up
where it circles against a dark sky,
and for a moment breaks the clouds
where starlight pours
into stillness,
a silence that veils
a people—visible—invisible,
who have always lived
who will always breathe
in the still
and sovereign
glory of life
worth living.

MAKING ALIYAH

Because we can think,
we are afraid of the dark.

~

At night, from the bottom bunk, in the middle of the '70s top ten, just after "Another One Bites the Dust," the radio light glowing against the blackness, I slide off my bed, get on my knees and give thanks that God made me, ask Him to help me understand why the screaming has to echo so loudly down the hall, why he has to call her that, why she can't be kind to him. I listen for my parents—Jewish kids don't pray like this—not hands folded like this and not on knees—something from TV. When the moon is full I can sometimes find my face imprinted on the surface, that the cosmic dust that strikes it formed the pattern of my life.

~

At 13, when they call me to the Torah, I speak in muted prayers sewn into me through countless afternoons with the Rabbi. No revelry, no celebration, just me, my father, the Rabbi, and 100 others looking on. I wait for manhood to come over me. I notice the women are upstairs, that the Rabbi's breath smells like coffee, that I am cold. After a while I look up into the stained glass near the temple ceiling waiting for a change to happen, some touch from the almighty, something to make it true. There is a feeling like being folded in half. By the end of the day, I make a promise that I will go to Israel.

~

She is young, brown hair in a straight fall from her baseball cap pulled tightly around her head. She's not tall, I can't see her eyes, but her lips are full, and her mouth moves softly.

She demands I follow her into hidden places, wander for years.

I spend my reality on her. She folds her hands in mine, pulls my fingers to her desperate face, spreads my palm on her cheek and gently guides it down softly along the smoothness of her neck, the rounds of her shoulders so warm beneath her uniform, my hand tracing the outline of her breast. This isn't my life.

We sit and talk about religion when it's late and she's already had a few glasses of wine.

We decide that it must be that every Christian must question eternity at least three times. More wine until we find ourselves agreeing that Adam and Eve are real, but single-celled, the Garden no bigger than a pinch of water. Evolution just as God had planned it.

~

One foot toward Mecca, one foot in the temple, one hand folded over prayer beads, the other in an open meditation. My mind is unfastened to the loudest voice. Reverence for life, sit beneath trees, find my chi, open my heart, big church doors and school cafeterias, there is not food enough for the hunger of God.

The seeds in our blood can't be dug out. They take root in the flow, sprout a thousand paths that we try not to follow. This is why I step off the plane into the place of dry bones. My hands close and open in the sun. I come here by a promise and find a covenant from sky to sky and earth.

THE SEEDPLANTER

On El Al from LA to Tel Aviv
the father stands.
He gives up his seat
while his little girl sleeps.
Together, they are a new chance.

His fingers are blocks of iron
that thud along the overhead bin.
His hands fully alive as
he bends his kippah
over smooth and thinning hair.
His arms are thick and full of hope.

I want his hands to level mine
to clench down, hold fast.
These are hands that move mountains.

I've been told
that to move mountains
I need only speak to them.
Just a seed of faith will do,

but his strength is silent,
my voice, weak and still.

I wonder how many seeds
the iron blocks have planted.
How much faith it has taken
him to work the land,
his muscle built from lost flesh
and long remembrance.

How do I appear to him?
Hiding behind wire and headphone,
a shy, silent wanderer.

I strain to hear the
davening of the Chasidim
up and back along the aisles.
I mutter these to myself
in quiet incantations
mouthing each desperate sound.

Then, on his knees cramped
in the aisle, head turned down,
he is also saying prayers.
His words are hushed,
"Hear O Israel . . . "
the familiar, rooted hum.

These are also my words,
and for a moment, the verse
moves together and away again,
slipping into some memory.

How different we are
    how the same
        the seedplanter and me.

When I look up,
his eyes are luminous
and full of me or
out the window.

BARIYET AL QUDS

On the road from Jerusalem,
going south toward Jericho,
the hills have turned green
from the winter rain,
and the sheep are fat
on the hillside. In the vales,
the Bedouin take tea
in the twilight
like they have
since before
this highway was built.
I am in a cab racing
toward Almog Junction.
Once there, I will cross into Jericho,
but for now the driver
says his visa will work.
He says that it should
allow him to make
it through both checkpoints.
If only by faith now,
I give the driver a date from Masada,
he offers me some juice from Gaza.
We half smile
and wait silently
for the checkpoints
where he hopes to make it over,
where I hope to make it over.
At the Israeli checkpoint
the guard is barely 19 and waves
us through with only a look.
There is time for a breath.
100 yards down the road,
a deep brown hand reaches
for my passport.
It rubs against his machine gun

as he steps away from us,
whispers into a radio,
and I wait as Jericho spreads out ahead of me.
There is wire, and camels, and mountains, and dust.
In the distance,
the banana fields are rising through the canyons.
By the time I get my passport,
the sun has moved behind the mountain.

CITY OF PALMS

There are none left who need a map.

In the Center of Jericho
the souk floods
in dates, bananas, citrus fruits,
men selling maps,
falafel stands and electronics.
I stand outside a stationary store.
A young girl browses colorful folders.
Her uniform is clean, and she is smiling
at the TV in the dusty window.
In the corner there are magazines with beautiful
people on the covers, cartoon characters
I have never seen, reams of paper
stacked to the ceiling.
Suliman makes copies of school notes,
a half shekel per page.
When the machine breaks down,
I hear yelling in Arabic,
guttural, elegant.
Outside I can smell the shwarma.
A man shouts from a car
at another man bent over, idle in the road.
Children run.
The sun beats down,
and midday echoes
with the prayers floating on thick air.
A man with one leg
is outside selling maps.
He follows the only other
who looks like me, a foreigner here.
He is trying to sell him a map,
only the map is five years old.
I know because I bought one earlier today.
Five years ago,
before the second fatwa,

Jericho was full of us,
our pockets lined with shekels,
day trips and tour buses
to see the world's lowest city,
the Elisha Spring,
the monastery,
and the Mount of Temptations.
Now the map is dead,
the City reborn.

AQBAT JABER

refugee camp, Jericho, West Bank, Israel

Black flags rise above open ceilings
mourning the death of Saddam Hussein,
and the streets are not streets
just dirt paths, dust rising inside my lungs.
Suliman teaches me to say *marhaba,*
welcomes me with this rounded word,
asks me to use it as a greeting,
and so I say it over and over to everyone I see.
Marhaba to the shy girl in the doorway with no building.
Marhaba to the Bedouin father
who invites us for chalky tea
and an afternoon bathed in blue smoke.
Marhaba to the mother who pulls her daughter closer in.
Marhaba to the goats,
to the group of young men,
sons of Palestine
who reach into themselves,
pull out their toughness,
wear it like a necklace,
only the chain is rusted and broken,
and I feel more sad than afraid.
Marhaba to the young kids
who clamor over my camera,
hold up peace signs,
make scary faces, and the little girls
who shy away laughing, running away
over and over.
Marhaba to Ahmed,
round as his soccer ball in his blue-hooded sweatshirt
of Che, looking tough even in the West Bank.
Marhaba from the depths of me
to the men at the mosque
with wisdom breath
and skin held together
by strife.

TWO HUNDRED FEET BELOW THE SEA

Aqbat Jaber Refugee Camp, West Bank, Israel

Banana farmers beg the sun
to be merciful.
Deep in the earth
water waits to spill up
into the dirt washes
that become baskets
of bottle green
filled with busheled
leaves grown wild
in the air of the Dead Sea.

The refugee town
buildings reach
brick by brick,
and I walk with Suliman
arm in arm,
beyond nervous,
    remembering
that I do not look Jewish
in a place where a notion
of this part of me
might cause me to disappear.
Secret streets deserted
to eyes used to busy streets
until behind one broken, red door,
framed into an unfinished heap
of cinder blocks,
        I see you
            little one
                staring at me,
and I smile.

I imagine the strains of you,
the split-hair-life
you lead in the quiet doorway.

It is hot today—in January,
here, in this bowl below the sea.
The scorching air packed in the door frame,
and you step back into the dark brick

What do you see?
This tall man
pale in the golden sun
away from who he is?

Can you have compassion for me?
Can you see hope,
not because of what I can bring you,
but because I might want to meet you?

I pause for a moment,
and Suliman looks at me
patient, curious.
What I want to say to her is,

Come out from behind that doorway—
be beautiful.
Live.
Live.
I want to ask you about
what it means to be alive in this place,
your home,

through wrecked gates
through viral water
through sheep's dung,
and black smoke,
the lonely caress of waiting.

But I say nothing
because I am afraid,
because in a place like this
I have no rights
just as she has no rights.

I turn to Suliman and ask him
if he knows this little girl.
He looks at the doorway,
smiles at the insignificance of my question.
He is not cruel, just my question
is so out of place in his experience.
He mumbles something in Arabic,
or maybe in English.

It will be later on
in the afternoon
at Suliman's house,
sharing stories,
taking tea along the wash
filled up with garbage,
the smell of honey
more rich than trash,
when I will see the tiny figure,
the long black hair
of the little girl
walking toward us,
keeping her distance
but still looking.
Even as I pretend
that I don't notice her,
her eyes turn me inside out.
        How did I get here?
                I remember a sensation of running in my legs,
                        dust in my eyes
                                                      thirst.

THE DIVIDING WALL

written on the dividing wall, Palestinian side, between Bethlehem and Jerusalem

"Face the wall with dark
closed gate, beat with bare brown fists . . ."
street prophets have
blown in blue spray
on the side
of the wall between
Bethlehem and Jerusalem.

No ordinary wall,
people walk into
the marketplace
clothed in bombs
and mindlessness
desperation
dressed in the hope
of something, anything
that might say "enough."

Mothers won't let their children
ride the bus to school
since the last intifada.
The streetcorner
is plaqued in bronze
with the Hebrew names
of blown-up children
because not everyone
wants peace
or understands the dry
enduring nature
of this torn place.
The checkpoints
are only hinges
rusty and fixed together

shrill at each opening.
The mouths
of the valleys
on either side have been shut.

A partition separates
tree from tree,
hill from hill.
A fence soars 25 feet up.
A barricade stomps
an elephant foot into the dry earth,
a concrete slab of blue and gray metal
threaded with razor vines
so immense it mutes all cries.

It is said that Herod built
Masada on a high plateau
in the Judean Wilderness
proving his devotion to himself.
This wall is not anointed
in the same way.

Here the bricks of the streets,
the rocks against metal and wire,
the sandstone and dry wind
sing for a new prophet
under the graffiti
bullseye "place bomb here."

How long can this wall protect
or hide away its people,
hold back the arms of the cities?
Not far away, the Temple wall
rises with the force of 5000 years.
Folded prayers stuffed into its cracks
balance centuries of weight.

In Bethlehem,
from the place where it is said

Jesus was born,
the wind gusts
through the Jerusalem gate
along the concrete barricade
on a faded watchtower
where in red spray paint
it says, “He wept.”

67TH AND 3RD

I stand outside
Park East Synagogue,
Yom Kippur.
I need to see.
I need to remember.

Men in dark suits
are dressed up today.
Women wear the same
black dresses that my grandma wore,
their heads covered in reverence.

I'm in my Quicksilver shirt,
torn jeans,
California flip flops,
backwards cap.
I am lost.

A huge man
waves a metal detector
as families come one by one
down the stairs.

I am homeless,
unlooked for.
I want to join them.
I want to show them
the certificate of my Bar Mitzvah,
my arms reaching
into imagined welcome.

At the end of the line,
a father shepherds his family,
his aged and spotted hands
on the back of his son's head,

helps him with his kippah,
small hands fold into the father's,
the children awkward in long suits.

A young mother
dressed in black
kisses her grandfather,
mouths "Shana Tova,"
her dark eyes shifting.
She is whispering to her daughters.
Her eyes meet mine and back again.
She searches my muted face,
my green shoulder bag filled with books
that tell the story of my new life,
but she doesn't know.
Her elegant hand pulls her daughters close.
I turn to spare them.
There are no more choices.
Along the street,
Synagogue at my back,
the light is in the west,
my prayers spilling out.

VIDUY (*CONFESSION*)
TESHUVA (*REPENTANCE*)

My Father's favorite High Holiday
was Yom Kippur
because it was here that he could perform
the quiet act of viduy,
the confession of his sins
to Hashem alone.
During the service
there is a time when
the Ark doors are held open
and the Torah scrolls are unrolled.
Grown men gather near
and murmur their darkest secrets.

We clean our hearts,
our minds,
our souls,
the best we can.
We carry ourselves there
in any way possible
with hope that Hashem will hear.
We've spent weeks making things right
with those we love and can't love,
our children, our brothers,
our parents and friends.
We make it right with G-d.
We pray the "Al Chet,"
we get to the root,
and as we pray we tap
our chests as an offering to G-d.

For the mistake we committed before You in public and in private.

It was different for my Father.
On these days there was unimaginable joy.

Rosh Hashanah had come, time
to ask G-d to write his name into the Book of Life.
For him this started when he would come home,
an enterprising young man who had gone out into the world,
22, full of life and owning every second of it.
He would be the hero of his shul, the one who would
leave and return to carry on the family name.
Even though he was always late to service,
even Kol Nidre,
the daylight just waning,
he would stride into synagogue
head high and shoulders back
holding his kippah to his head.
The Rabbi would look up,
and after a long pause shake his head
and say, "Oize, go kiss your bubby."
He knew he was welcome.
Accepted.

Before Yom Kippur,
his Bubby's house,
the hottest day of fall,
would be filled
with the faces from the neighborhood,
all generations of women,
wearing high heels and black dresses,
speaking in different tongues,
wishing Shana Tova,
the men in their finest suits
smelling of camphor balls
and cigarette smoke.
In the kitchen,
my father fed
on cheese blintzes
seltzer and orange jelly
smiling at his grandmother.
"These were the days," he would tell me.
"This is when I knew what it was like to come home

before 1960, the divorce,
when the family used to talk to me."

For the mistakes we committed before You by exercising power.

It was on the days before Yom Kippur
we felt the anticipation.
These were the High Holidays,
and children under 13 were not allowed to fast,
but we did not have to go to school either.
We had to stay apart from the drinking fountain
and fruit juice. While other kids played dodge ball
and football on the concrete playground of P.S. 6,
we weren't allowed to go.

We wanted to fast like our parents and grandparents.
We wanted to make them proud of us,
but mostly I was only curious
why the darkness sat on top of my house
and my parents would walk around muttering the names
of loved ones and lost ones.
I was curious about why my grandmother,
who would call me everyday
say, "Christopher, how are you?"
her smile glowing through the phone
would, on this day, not even talk to me.
I could hear her long sobs through the receiver
swimming into my father's head,
a begging, and then a mash
of Yiddish and English and Hebrew stewed together,
a real toomel: a noisy chaos,
"Oy gevald!" and "A chaleyre,"
then a long wailing through the phone,
my father dragging on his Kool Filter Kings.
"Okay, okay, okay," over and over,
and then, "I'm sorry,
I'm sorry,
Sorry."

I hid in my room and played Atari.

When my father got off the phone,
I asked him why he was so upset.
He told me that this was the Day of Atonement,
that this was the day the gates of heaven were open
and that men and women were to ask G-d for
forgiveness and be written into the Book of Life,
even men like him.

He half-smiled at me,
walked into the kitchen,
and I went back to my room.
I couldn't know what it would have meant to atone,
but I did understand guilt,
so I stood in my bedroom
and asked G-d to forgive me for playing Atari
on the Holiest of Holy days.

After my Bar Mitzvah,
before my father left us for another woman,
he came to me on Yom Kippur,
scooped his stained palm behind my neck—
"Happy New Year, you mensch. You did it.
This year your name is being written in the Book of Life,
and this year you fast from sunset to sunset, atone for your sins,
and ask G-d to forgive you."
But I didn't feel like I had done anything wrong.
He seemed more excited than me,
his face swollen with hope and desperation
alive again in me.
Maybe he knew then that in a few months he would leave us.
Maybe he thought that if he could push this truth into me now it would last.
Maybe he knew then that he would have so much to atone for
in the years behind,
in the years ahead.

For the mistakes we committed before You through confusion of the heart.

And this is why we tap our chests.
This is where most of it comes from,
confusion of the heart.
And on this holiest of Holy Days,
I am looking around for the Ark
with its doors open.
I am asking God to forgive me for the confusion of my heart.
I am asking it all the way back to the ones who left Egypt.
I am asking it all the way back to the ones who wandered
to the shores of the Jordan and across.
I am asking it all the way back to my ancestors in Romania.

I am asking it all the way back
to my grandmother,
and my father,
and me.
I am asking it all the way back
to the ones who never made it.
I am saying,
Baruch atah Adonai, Eloheinu, melech ha-olam
seven times.
I am looking around for the Ark,
and the scrolls in the Ark,
the Torah laid out before me,
the gates of heaven
before they are locked.

I am crying out for the gates to stay open long enough for me to ask
for forgiveness all the way back to the beginning of it all.
And I am seeing my father and I sitting in the desert
in the bright sun, and he is crying and telling me he is sorry
for all of it. He is making me promises that he means to keep,
and I believe him.
There is the smell of bloodstained olive wood
or cedar—it is my Father.
It is the hand in my hand that won't let go.
It is a lion's breath in my ear that whispers softly,
        It is finished.

OF ELK AND MARRIAGE

Pt. Reyes Station, Tule Elk Preserve

At Tomales Point, above the bay,
I hold my wife's hand. She is quiet
again, lost again, deep within her
brown skin, hiding from the eczema.
She has not slept for days. The itching
mostly comes at night, and these same hands
which bless and love and hold, become blades
in cracked and earthy skin, but today
she is trying to be a fine wife.

The truck shifts slowly along the edge
of the windy road through the Tule
Elk Preserve. Hunted for one hundred
years until ranchers found a remnant,
gave the elk space and time
to find each other again through shy
wandering, a quiet faith and purpose.

I search for them across rolling grass
where redwoods tower in distant groves,
and storm clouds press into the valleys,
the truck window fogged in saltwater
blown from Point Reyes. The elk appear from
a stand of trees. Rain is falling in the meadow.
I pull to gravel, turn off the car.
Silent, she looks at me, her eyes cruel
with pain and obligation.

"What?" she says,
"Look," I say, and spot a bugling male.
He is gathering in his harem,
collecting as many cows as he can.
"Amazing." I hold my hand on my mouth
in awe. She's staring at me,

the air in the truck is lost, sucked out.
Her eyes are not her own.
My eyes are not my own.
It is this moment under a cold
and quiet sky we lose
who we think we are.

Husband? Wife?
In sudden and dire warmth
I open the door to bitter air,
and she shivers, "I hate this."
Her hands recoil. Her body constricts.
The rain batters us into talking
of our new marriage, nature, love,
promises and expectations of a fresh life.
Elk walk across the wet plain.
We are far from what we understand.

She takes off her wedding ring, slips it
through slender fingers in tight circles.
Months before, in Moorea
on our honeymoon,
I waited on a motu watching
in my blue trunks, snorkel in my hand.
From the small island I saw
her sitting curled up beneath the hut,
her skin darkened beneath a wide hat.
That morning I convinced her to try
to go into the water, promised
her that saltwater is mild
in the South Pacific, and
it would not sting her broken skin.
Desperate, unable to touch her,
I thought the vision of the reef would
remind her of her strength. The water
burned more than my false promise.

Her skin is worse now, welted over.
Hushed in our disagreement we wait

for our commitment to work.
What did I expect of her?
Her brown eyes blistered in the storm.

I leave the truck, climb the rise,
let myself fall into the far country.
This is what I understand: the sky,
the elk, the sea beyond, and the rain.
This was not my prayer, a life
with her, or anyone else.
I never believed in marriage
or the truth of faithfulness,
until the night we first met,
our slow push and pull of fingertips,
hands folding into rest unlooked for.

There is a burning in my legs,
sudden air between the bay and sea.
I feel I might somehow turn to grass,
that she may never change, never see this,
or care, never be better again.
The elk bull watches while cows graze.
The rut season has come on.

When I walk toward the truck, the window
is rolled down, the rain blows in,
her arm is wet and alive.
Her hand is reaching for me—
an unexpected gesture.
I slowly fit it into mine.
I'm slipping in the gravel.
Across the road, an elk calf
stands in the treeline watching us.

MOUNTAIN LIONS

Penciled outlines
of big cats
warn the trail
at the base of the mountain.
Stonewall Peak aches
in my legs. Perfect
bleached, granite peaks,
long flat, overlook,
the desolation of Borrego,
the spine of the Lagunas,
the ravens spun in a high loft
marking the peak.
Distrustful watchers,
I ignore them and linger
on the rock face,
lost in some blue-sky-dream.

Later, along the loose path
manzanitas burst,
oaks bend and pitch
back and back
in a wind rush,
push me against
stone and tree,
and I forget myself
in the absurdity
of my own thoughts,
the pervasive remembrance
of things to do.
My legs are weary
my mind, lost on the winding path
down and down
mellowed by the sun.

When I see her, I remember
the world is not mine.
Quietly in the hills above Cuyamaca,

a thing out of legend has come,
forgotten, unreal,
in uneven breaths,
her ears branched delicately
along the brush,
her shoulders pressed
tightly into her forepaws,
the sharp gape and yawn and stretch
in the coolness of tree and trail.

I fold myself, curl tightly,
my elbows over my knees,
remember that I am never to do this
if I see a lion, but it has taken
thousands of trustful steps,
and years of silence and waiting
to meet her, so I risk it.

Time slips between us until
a quiet blow of animal air
pushes against earth,
and after a time,
sinewy legs
bending in the sunlight
turn her up the rocks
and out of sight.
The air is thick
with the absolute truth
of the creature.

Beneath the oaks I linger
for a long time, watched over,
smelled out, searching for a way
to remain lost here in this twilight truth
until the wind brings
the laughter of children
coming down the trail above me
and faithful to my own I confess,
"There's a mountain lion in the trees." I whisper to them,
"We must try to seem larger than we really are."

A PRAYER FOR CUYAMACA

Cedar Fire, 2003, San Diego

The oaks are gone, the pine trees burnt out matchsticks. The first pain comes from all of the sun on the road where the shade of those oaks would filter the light onto the pavement. Rolling green hills are broken by coughs of blackened rocks and stumps, and in the pits of the valleys are branches, debris, and deer bones piled up and set to burn in a deliberate way. Stonewall Peak is bald, an old man shrinking down. where once there was a forest, now the mountain is exposed—not a tree, not a single tree left to comfort him. Across the road, up Cuyamaca Peak, the oracle of the forest, the centuries-old fairy-tree, is gnarled into ash. The road up to Middle Peak, the one along the fast stream, a window through to the meadow is browned now, an empty field of desolation burnt by some angry dragon breath. Oaks and pine scatter into small fertile valleys. No more long view, only pockets of new life. It will never be the same. No voice can chant the trees into rising, or the waters to flow more deeply, or the lions to come out of hiding, or raise the dead buried in their trunks. But even though the deer that filled the forests were swept up by some great hand, hiding now in unreachable places, hushed signs of their return, hoof prints and droppings mark the dirt beneath my shoes. It will start again. Hope already seeps into the soil, pushing yellow and purple up and out, and there are some meadows, far and green in the long sun, and a prayer now, a quiet plea for Heaven to let in a little more of itself on to the Earth.

SAN DIEGO ZOOLOGICAL SOCIETY

for Sami

The zoo is the church.
There is no other hope
except this place
set aside to remember
how life should look.
When I bring my children
to show them what the world
is like in custom ecosystems
"Tiger River," "Ituri Forest,"
even in their joy
they sense the cruelty,
not old enough yet
to understand why
all things are not free.

And still, yesterday
you saw your first
meercat, that snarling
and famed rodent.
You grunted loudly
your face vibrating,
finger pointing.
Your older brother and I
looked at you, at each other,
and we knew that the zoo
was our frontier,
but that maybe it is really your place
as you grunt and beam
through otters, pigs,
and kit foxes,
and I can't help but think
about how much more
you are a "you" like no other,
and each animal too,

that you see a hope here, invite us
back into something
that is not entirely lost.

acumen

for Caylao

Have you seen the tortoise move?
One oblong foot scrapes cement
the other pulled along,
the desperate stretch of the neck
probes the air.
Thick eyes blink two by two.
Children stand on cage bars,
look down on the enclosure
from a high vantage point
"A turtle! A big ol' turtle!"
The turtle pees.

A tortoise sighs, it really does,
grunts uncontrollably,
the air curling steam before its nostrils
the nails held back by skin
the plated helmet
and the shell,
the impenetrable shell
imposes and protects,
the easy retreat,
the burden of safety
carried forever.
The tortoise   does not see distance
or the future
the food is along the way,
the food is roots dug in,
side by side
torn up, dropped off, uprooted.

They don't think to hunt,
scrounge as they move
pod to pod,
shrunken in their shells

or limbs extended beyond purpose.
They stop among each other.
It must be warm
where the shells
slide together like bricks.

THE PARK

for Asa

You love the park
when kids play
beneath the pepper trees
swinging, climbing
sliding through the tunnel.
Very brave of you,
and a new development
because you don't like dark places
since you figured out
the strangeness of the dark.
We wait for Lorien,
Joaquin, Jack, and
others you call
by name,
sometimes by color
"my orange friend."
It doesn't matter
because they're your friends.
You try and share
and often can't,
except for moments
of divine kindness
where you give
the car to the crying boy,
your "purple friend."
He needs it.

SNOOLS

This morning,
you called me in
at 5:30,
told me
you had found
a snool.
Your tiny,
two-year-old hands
held open,
lifted up
before your
smiling, sleepy face.
"What color is it?"
I asked.
"It's a blue one."
In this early light
your eyes bright
and almond
like your mom's,
you looked like
someone from a dream,
a boy I might hope to know,
who'd imagine
snools, share them
with me when you could.
"I dropped it!" you said,
and looked down,
threatened tears,
but this is part of the life
of snools.
They are often dropped
and found again.

SAMARIA

Before you were born,
I whispered
into your mother's womb
that your faith will
be the strongest of all,
that you'll know
what truth tastes like
and have nothing else.
When I look at you,
your deep eyes are holding me,
your miniature finger
pointing at me
waiting for mine.
I see that you already know
when your father
is lost, that he has wandered
outside into the night air
to catch his breath.
Already you bring me back
to the courageous
patting of outstretched hands,
your feet up
reclining in your high chair
so you can see your foot,
your lips pursed into a smile.

WHAT NOW IS BEAUTY?

Am I allowed to ask this?
Most days I think of my son
standing still in the open
green and yellow field,
the house pushed against
a complex forest.
I am looking toward the road.
He is behind me picking
weeds, stuffing them into his
pockets, scratching up his hands.
He is asking questions now,
What is at the end of space?
How was God here before He was born?
The field reddens into the sunset,
and my son is standing there along my legs.

It isn't that there is anything to fear,
all is as it has been and will be.
The sun changes the shape of the house
as it sets. The trees surrender
their form to the moon.
It is in this moment, just before it gets dark,
I see the clouds are stepping on him,
casting their long shadows,
and I pull him into me,
lift him up with a father's hands.
I need him to know the difference
between his own legs and mine.
I want him to feel the air
as his legs go skyward,
and his weight is not his own.
I need him to know
that the space between his feet and the land
is where the world happens.
I lift him high so he'll forget the ground.

SHABBAT

Shabbat candles flicker even as I load the dishwasher
in direct violation of Talmudic law.
Quiet at last, I cover the challah and drink the wine from the kiddush cup.
The children sleep with songs on their lips,
and the crickets have begun.
On the kitchen wall, there is a picture of my father
standing in the desert, looking west in his cowboy hat,
one of his best days before he died. I whisper, "We keep the Sabbath now,"
a jewel of tradition carried back from Israel.

A year ago, in Jerusalem, on the Sabbath, our friend Ameil
looked across the table, whispered as if the secret must not get out,
"Hebrew is about symbols, the language of the heart.
Bitter herbs, candles, the eye, the bush, the sea, the temple, the Sh'ma,
there is no room, for these symbols are in the life of the mind
that pours over books, reaches into proofs by paper and scrolls,
by dig and chemical."
Ameil smiled and spread his hands across the cedar table.
"Remember the Sabbath," he said. "Keep it holy. Find the symbols."
January in Jerusalem, standing on the roof near the Old City,
the stars are bursting over Bethlehem, and I am talking on the phone
to my father making him promises he does not deserve.

I remember tonight plate by plate,
the irreverent and wonderful chaos,
my daughter's Hello Kitty dish
swimming in butter and honey.
My son's plate is clean. He ate it all
even though his bottom never touched
the chair, his legs dancing from uncle
to grandmother through every loving
and biting reprimand, his face gleaming
in the silver salad bowl.

My mother, each Friday, her Jewishness awakened,
tells stories of Greenwich Village and briskets past, her plate picked at,

her fork wandering from rice to lettuce to hummus and back;
lonely olives swim in soaked bread and spilled wine.
She looks for my father, eats in terms of him,
longs for the ferocity of his youth, and even later
when he could no longer get the food to his mouth.
My brother fingers his phone, eats.
He is searching for God in every bite,
quiet in his wondering,
afloat in Sabbath peace.
And my wife finally sits down,
each bite separate, perfected
into magnetic clusters from every side of the platter.
The baby is asleep now in her arms.

The candles burn in the twilight kitchen,
and I linger above the lights until the wax spreads itself
into paraffin heaps, a quiet like walking in the woods.
The mess is the symbol, the still small voice,
these empty plates, sweeping the floor,
the loveliness of her hands kneading the bread,
twisting it with the children hand in hand in the late afternoon.
This a real thing, something permanent, a cord tied from this kitchen
from the table leg to cedar, acacia, clay, and brush.
There are times worth remembering.
The story of this night has happened before,
the beginning of impractical rest and impossible forgiveness.
If we can just do *this*, I think, we can make it.

THE BROOM TREE

When Elijah left Beersheba, he wandered until he found a broom tree and sat beneath it, told God, no more. He knew enough to remember truth even in his misery. That truth, the broom tree, the angel, all that he had seen and all that he had left somehow wrapped itself together to be the voice of God.

In my backyard,
the pomegranate
bursts with fruit
reddening into September.
I look beneath its branches every day
for a smooth spot to sit.
I am losing my strength
in this world.

Beneath the broom tree, Elijah ate the last of his bread, drank until his wineskins bled dry, and laid his head down on a rock. The stillness calmed him. He was afraid, not for the first time, and he saw her face in the very sky, and he could not escape the fear. Her beauty terrible like cold starlight, Jezebel, her voice melodic, her power complete, and the sweat in his eyes burned him. He slept there for a very little while, the tortured sleep of dread.

All at once,
I understand
with each day
I live less and less
for myself.

It is only in loneliness that a man can fully join forces with the devil.
Elijah began to imagine prayer, his self-pity overflowing now into the
dry and coarse air. "Take my life O Lord,
I'm like my Fathers before me!"
It was at this moment that the branches of the broom tree moved over
his body, the leaves translucent, almost white in the sunlight,
and there, near the rock, the impossible smell of hearth cake.

But this is not some noble revelation.
It's an unavoidable circumstance
where nobility sometimes rises
here. Under the leafy branches
of this pomegranate,
I wonder if quietly
angels are close.

He ate and drank from an earthen jug, and again he lay down, his fear dimmed, his strength flowing back, and his breath even and true with the unmistakable shake of some heavenly hand. He filled his body with remembrance and hope folded into holy fear. He sat up, leaned against the tree and looked out across Judah. Horeb appeared in the distance. Below the hill of the broom tree, blackness seeped into the desert floor. Elijah walked.

But if there are angels,
they won't always talk to me,
or I can't hear the voices
quiet in the cold.
My feet are broken, weak now.
I've been waiting for twenty-five years
to find a place where the trees are thick
where both mountains and oceans meet,
and not a city or a town, but a village,
quiet, loyal, the buildings made of wood.
A place to live,
move away from
and come back again.

To walk forty days with no shoes was not the difficult part. It was the spears and arrows of Jezebel that were the greatest obstacle. The angel had commanded he go, and Elijah believed him, but her words about the sword and the truth of death of all the prophets at her hand filled him with an earthly fear. Perhaps, he thought, beneath the moon one night, this is why He is making me walk all the way to Horeb. Forty days beneath the sun. Forty days under the cold moon.

The backyard door is open
and inside my children are laughing,
calling each other by name.
Already they are covered in crayon
and oatmeal, apples and mismatched clothes.
They are waiting for me
in the simple joy of a new morning,
bread from the toaster,
coffee poured.

All of it tries
to bring me back
to some kind of truth,
catching sunfish in the pond,
Catskill summer,
or a torn sun dress
after a long day at the shore,
or when the days get busy,
and my wife's been gone for hours,
I still feel her body when the sheets are cold,
and I drink her half-glass of water.

Yet even at Horeb, at the heart of his journey, Elijah hid in a cave,
filled with fear, asking for his very life, full of obedience. Listening.

Under the shadow of this tree,
I feel this cave.
I understand its embrace.
I lived inside its rocky walls
for so many years.
I've hoped for earthquakes, for wind, for fire,
and I'm ready now,
to hide my face in leaves,
to hear the still small voice, "Why are you here?"

And I will answer honestly now,
the truth now.

The ground shakes the roots of the tree.
I am standing at the entrance to the cave,
and I am full of hope.
I know why
I was made
to walk this far.
I am ready.
I am afraid.
I am listening.

Acknowledgments

There are so many people to thank for their love and support of me as a writer and a human being. Thank you to my parents who chose an extraordinary life and made me go with them. To my brother who never gives up. My teachers, mentors, and friends who have sat and listened to every crazy idea and all my words sewn together; Sandra Alcosser, Glover Davis, Marilyn Chin, and many others through all the years. My MFA conspirators, Phillip Hu, Matt de La Peńa, Matt, Sydney, Vicki and others. Thank you to my true family from Coast Vineyard and Dwell who have carried me (and my family) through all the "real" stuff of life. My beloved friends, Maggie Flack, Emmet Blue, Hope and Chris Herrera, Alan Traylor, Randy Hasson, John and Michelle Hundley, Jeff and Kristine Magee, Mike Hettinger, Chris Whyte, Casey Whitsett, Jamie and Michelle Wilson, Mike Marchesini, Sean Lockhart, Jamie Wilson, all of the Blues, Steph, Olivia, Lisa, Natalie, Doug, Jess, and now I am stumbling into so many names, but you all are dear. Thank you to my mentors, Don Williams, Bob and Lauren Hasson, John Block, Jack Webb, and a handful of others. My friends at the CS Lewis Foundation for always inspiring me to remember that I am the "Trucker Poet." My colleagues whom I am so privileged to work with, Kelly Mayhew, Jim Miller, Cathy Harlow, Aileen Gum, Gavin Brown, Meagan Marshall, Dr. Adey Stembridge, and so many others whom I aspire to be more like. Thank you, of course, to my English Center family. And thank you to the authors of this book, Heather Eudy, Cali Linfor, and Sabrina Youmans, who have been brilliant and loving companions on this journey. You have breathed life into me. And finally, thank you to my family: Ella, for her love, companionship, and inspiration. My son Asa (healer), who reminds me that "it is easy to write books," my daughter Samaria (guard on the mountain), for her devotion to her daddy, and my daughter Caylao (fellow lightbearer), who was born as this book was being written. All of you are the reason.

Notes

Many thanks to the editors of the following publications where these poems first appeared.

Aethlon: The Journal of Sport Literature, Fall 1995. "Waking the Boats." Johnson City Tennessee: East Tennessee State University Press.

Pearl, Fall/Winter 1997. "Origins." Long Beach, CA.

Poudre Canyon Cache, January 1999. "Civilization Case." Sierra Club Press, Colorado.

Broken Bridge Review, October 2007. "The Language of Rivers."

San Diego Writer's Ink Anthology of San Diego Writers, 2010. "Aqbat Jaber."

Mamas and Papas, 2010. "The Park." City Works Press.

Border Voices Poetry Anthology, 2011. Featured Poet, "Dog Hill," "Origins."

Charlotte Literary Review, 2011. "The Green Box."

This Time Not Alone, 2011. "Life Unworthy of Living," "Samaria," "Origins."

Bills of Lading

Heather Eudy

To the Reader

In the literal sense, a "bill of lading" is a receipt exchanged upon delivery of goods or services. In the early 2000s, I made my living delivering vehicles. The labor involved picking up cars (run-of-the-mill company sedans and nondescript white medical vans) and driving them to their assigned destinations, anywhere in the continental United States. Delivery of a vehicle always required a bill of lading. While the job was ultimately unsustainable (I slept in these cars in truck stop parking lots, had no guarantees I'd get a gig, and ended up on Greyhound bus rides I paid for myself more often than I engaged in gainful employment), I encountered a lot of road and a few strangers, for which I will always be grateful. Not long after, I lived in Mexico for a time.

Bills of Lading represents a series of poems (written before, during, and after being employed as a driver) that serve as metaphorical receipts—documents that record desire, isolation, connection, the creative process, travel, home, the spiritual journey, and hopefully a little bit of humor. These bills lade—they baptize, afflict, haul freight, and excavate. They are reckonings, announcements, and grievances. My offerings.

Contents

BILLS OF LADING

receipts exchanged upon delivery of goods or services

I believe there exists a universal truth that when you want something, you will not get it. Or is it that it is no longer yours? As though your fight for it withdrew it, released it for somebody else more qualified.

Like this table for instance. I drove into the Sunset Point Rest Area parking lot, off the 17 North to Flagstaff, and witnessed the perfect table, round and still aglow above the valley. I muttered, "Nobody better get that one." As I arranged my things to carry from the Taurus—notebook, cigarette, beverage—another sedan pulled up beside me from which a couple emerged. First they meandered toward a different site as I approached "mine" eagerly, when I sensed they saw it too and veered in my direction. I would have beaten them to it, but I asked in all good conscience, "Did you want that spot?" "Yes," the woman replied.

And don't they look perfect huddled before it at the cliff's edge?

I wonder what would have happened if I had taken the table. Would the next couple—the blonde in blue and the man with a camera—have lost their quintessential love trip photograph? Discontented, I'm a table behind and the tan ones laugh, gesture to the view, and will forever remember Sunset Point Rest Area, off Interstate 17. Or they will forget it until the blonde in blue thumbs through a worn album and thinks about the time the two were once one.

I'll let them embrace and I'll ponder other life forms like the cows across the asphalt munching in humdrum bliss. I'll have storms to watch for and stray tire bodies that gave in to the wear and the force of a trucker's hunt. Is there any money to be made out here? All drivers wonder. Jagged wishbone lightning, the water scoured this Ford of bugs, 4x4, 10x10. How many had a Kingman's highway burial?

I try to believe in the random draw of three hippie boys, topless, to the table now. They acquire their own beltless romance. One stands, stretches, slowly rubs down his chest—this will be his sex for the night. And mine.

RESERVATION PRICES

Signs determine
when we enter and when we leave
native regions
as if we could really
post boundary, name
which
Earth
  is
whose.

Somehow in travel
we understand the highway as sacred mesa
understand we can sit, lie down, walk even
and know our holy foundation.
Maybe history spins
too fast.
So we must drive our cars to be caught encircled
in its net. We are enmeshed.

We tell by billboard—jewelry
crafted in the fingers of
real, live
Indians.
Stones sell at *Reservation Prices.*
Two words that should never
have needed to be paired.
I wish I knew which tree unknowingly
gives up her body for my inky
(il)literate pen.

EVERYTHING MOVES IN PAIRS

the fluttering young barn owls
the bedraggled crows
the lanky wild geese
the snails cannibalizing each other

in embrace such wondrous

opaque owl wings
purple-black crow frames
goosenecks seeking sky, distance,
the snail shells dissolving, so too the trail

my mark, though, unnaturally
solitary scans the horizon
for comfort, maybe, or inspiration
but keeps coming up

two clouds, two oaks, two
shades of blue

HORSESHOES

At the furthest extension for tourists
inside the Grand Canyon, Phantom Ranch,
my father and brother flung these lucky rings
through black clouds and mist.
I must've been in my bunk
counting cellulite pockets.

At a birthday party, the men—
shoes in one palm, beer bottles in the other—
made real sport of throwing metal into dust
and tossed these boomerangs that thud,
don't fly, into the front yard.
Wives and children stayed indoors.

But I've held these helixes, too, traced
the folded rim. Heavy in the hand.
Who first thought a wounded circle, a moon
eaten away would be attracted to a spear,
a nail whose head is stuck in the ground?
And what does the horse have to say
about it all? Tell us about the surgery.
Most scars take this shape, a crescent
flick of the scalpel.

BELTWAY

an ars poetica, for the armadillo

Roadland creature, I dive
from the highway to the side
where you wait, watch the traffic,
where the miles swivel in armored
bands along the path around
the stomach to the back.

Fingers first, I force my hands
to probe your shell wound in spires.
Knuckles run from the plating
to the ink-sap in the veins,
to the low soft shoulder. And I start
with these phalanx bones
but soon the very rounds
of my heels have entered
and you close up with me
like I'm the last segment of a centipede
sucked inside your toothless mouth.

Waist and knee, shin and spine
all somersaulting from the roots
of your digging toes
to the crescent of your forehead.
Sprung to the top.
Prostrate. I lose track
of the entrance as your body
becomes a circle. Still swimming,
I'm in the center of you—
        shell and corrugated skin.

BETRAYED IN A SWIMSUIT

The sulfur you left in my swimsuit our last week together, Paso Robles,
no vinegar or baking soda or bleach could expunge
wafts up two-years-plus, suit long since discarded
a pungent ancient geyser, a hope & memory scramble still active
in ways tourists don't understand. But they're taking pictures.
And they're holding their noses.

GETTING CHASTISED BY JOHN LEE HOOKER

for Ronnie, a driver from Chicago who relieved me in Wichita

The letters roll and slur like Chicago, like all
the Sundays of loneliness, this Sunday
I can't get John Lee Hooker out
of my head

Serve you right to suffer
Serve you right to be alone

I don't want John Lee Hooker out of my head,
he belongs here, will likely never leave here,
I'm still singing:
I want you, cruel forgetter, tormenter, distance
maker, perfect one

Serve you right to suffer
Serve you right to be alone

It looks like I haven't
done this before, copied the arch of I want you,
your hollow limbs wrapped around my shape,
my sweet untenable slinky

Because you're still livin'
In days done past and gone

John Lee Hooker won't stop reminding me, please
don't stop reminding me, I've been here before,
like this road, I've always been here, this one that leads me to
Chicago, I'm still here, an imbecile with a prescription

For milk, cream and alcohol
He place me on milk, cream and alcohol

POST-NICOTROL

I've got a pattern down for this routine
of shelling seeds at night. They break beneath
my anxious hands and teeth replacing smoke
with dusty food. Substitute flower meat
for cigarettes. Supplant grandmother's scotch.
Here all I need are mouth and sound, a seed
that opens willingly and dries my tongue.
A paper plate receives the shells I've emptied
spread out like scabs, like fingernails. Disgust.
Temptation. Both attract a habit's birth.
I touch myself and dig into the bag,
my muddy palms caked thick with ashy earth.
I draft my right leg's shape, then zig and zag
across a length of thigh an alphabet
inscribed in denim, drawn by thumb and nail.
Though numb and motionless, I'm newly wet,
out of breath. I cup a fallen entrail
and slide it to the floor with the same hands
that stiffen at my crotch, that arch for more.
My toes pick the seeds out of carpet strands
a little sticky, flecked with white and blue.
I reach into the bag and break the home,
the hard skin of a body eaten through.

IF I DIDN'T HAVE TO CATCH THIS BUS

I would be on my way to Kansas City
listening to mixes made for wanting.
I would be on the side of the highway
at a rest stop smoking Winstons to the filter.
I would be having road thoughts, checking
my mirrors, anticipating the emptiness
of a gas tank—*hold out, little one,*
hold out a little longer.
I would enter twilight depression
and emerge giddy around midnight.

Dusk's easier in this gray
seat striped rainbow down the middle
and if I didn't have to catch this bus
I would not have made the acquaintance
of the hairy-chested man on Valium
riding to Dayton, offering me
beef jerky and gum.
I wouldn't have given a cigarette
and advice to Joe outside the station
who's starting over, got a job working trash,
sleeps at the shelter once dark enough to enter,
gave it all up—his wife, the drugs,
his home—because he'd *done wrong.*
He's at the bottom but hasn't
given up his beer. In time.

Mostly, I would not have subtly
flirted with an unemployed engineer
going home to grandbabies in Springfield,
shyly resting his lips on his bag
as he paused.
Wide open minutes—more
they've given me of themselves
than the ones whose beds I've shared.

Ohio's Mad River will be lit up
in moon later, the engineer
like a timid fisherman and I
looking on, casting into surfaces
with the softest of stones.

DENVER LULL

I have new eyes for Colorado tonight.
A mountain region where young fathers
discuss their babies and their music
unafraid of fingering Led Zeppelin songs
on patched and stickered caseless
guitars—*Why need a case*
when you're just gonna play?
To the passengers on the vacant bus, we
who missed the first one that came along.
Late, yes, later than the rest. And just in time
for sunset. For red cherry billboards.
Still got a few days now before home.
Eighteen-wheelers pull around the ramp while
we rock in mid-Colorado lullaby. And I
don't need a baby to make me sing.

HOPE CONDOMS

Stopped at Walgreen's
on the way home,
a misty night party return
for acetaminophen.

There they were—condom
packages a little past cosmetics,
Trojan ribbed, Xtreme, delayed
climax. The greatest gesture of
optimism I've made in a decade:
my pause here.

I chose a box.
A simple, understated Lifestyles
Ultra Sensitive. In smaller print
almost like wearing nothing
at all navy blue, green highlights.

I have no partner. None
foreseeable. But now or at least tonight
in this dark Sunday mist
I believe.
Lover, whoever you are,

whether in Berlin or Ben Gurion
or in my own town, an object
of pixilated photographs and drunken
embrace or another whose name I haven't yet
uttered, whose eyes I haven't yet sought,
whose frame waits in a somewhere doorway
for my fingertips.

Lover, lover, whoever you are,
I just bought a 12-pack of Lifestyles Ultra
Sensitive. Tell me your fly is undoing.

HOW COULD YOU DO THAT TO THE POMEGRANATE?

What exploitation the pomegranate has known,
frustrated hands carving her in sloppy thrusts.

They want her seeds. They crave her juice, use
her properties for the dogma of 613 Commandments.

And the symbol of fertility, a haunting shape
for women over 48, shriveling on the leaf.

The stuff of prostate health, plumping
in her filtered watery state.

Two girls bite into her in a river
bed, faces stained red.

OVULATION IN THE MARGINS

I cramp
in silence
twitching
discreet

one
of few
American
women
proclaiming
this
palpable

English won't
say it

so I turn
my tongue
to
Mittelschmerz

German names
before
numbing

while my
certain
fragrant
fever beguiles
grocery store

clerks

this
still
fertile
customer

BOCA DEL CIELO

Tonight I ask, in the girth of a hammock,
in the mouth of heaven,
am I still a writer?
Or is that a thing to which you cannot put an end?
I can tell you the moon
made a silly face at me
while I was watching,
and I can hear the breakers
from this sand spot dangling
mi pesado.

Thank you, wooden posts, a los menos
you don't mind my weight.

On the radio is something good
and Blanca's voice continues as she helps us all
find comfort in nylon and cueros.
I am ready for the sleep of cervezas,
small boat tours, herons, the bulb out here flickering,
the cabaña squealing y la pareja—las nuevas llegadas who keep
drinking coronas—and one corona for Eva, for her birthday.

Thank you, Eva, for your help with my hammock
and for hearing out my story.
Para servirte.

I wrote *A Dentro de las Olas* in the sand and we all
had something solitary to say in the moonlit
playa where waves continue
their interminable dance. In the morning,
we will hear the lanchas like today. Juanito took me
al otro lado and it was Miguel Angel, walking with crutches,
who guided us to the pelicans and other seabirds,
who helped pluck the splinters from my feet.

To write is to remember and to tell is to give.
Will I wonder the worth of my words
in this world off and on like white and black.
I think there's a star inside
the gap of the palmed shelter.
It's blinking out its chiapaneca light.

THE THIRD RAIL

the choice

the lack thereof

or hope might help here if hope if a persistent hope

but the third rail

runs along the red line

two steps east

then rapture

DEPENDENT VARIABLE

Can't I come over again tonight?
I'll choose to be inhaled, persuaded,
devoured, but even this is fantasy
since I'm the one asking you
to spread my wings apart,
fidget with me like entomologists do.
Fragile as paper, durable as reed,
I'm the skin, the hide of insect strength,
the better breed for analysts like you
who buckle incising external length.
I'll acquiesce if you undress
your labcoat, your spectacles, all the tools
that make me stay below the pins
heaving as though alive.

ON REDEFINING ASS

Sometime last night, in my single bed,
someone I thought might be God, if God
could be, spooned me between dreams,
caressed my fading hair spineward
all the way to the tailbone, and above
bleached sheets, pressed
with corporeal weight
against my ass.

I hate to say just ass. This thing has a mind
of its own. I promise you.
God knows this. God put the word out.
In the beginning was the Word. Ass divines.
Ass moves mountains. Ass deserves
a hymn, a march, a purgation offering,
a libation offering, meal
offering, incense offering,
blood offering,
sin.

IMAGING THE DIVINE

I.

A eunuch jiggling the leftover.
He held his long white hand
acast my head. Until it boughed
and I became a tree and the taste
of earth coming up from a rain
grew stronger than his untouched hand.
One bud caressed him and he collapsed
inside me as memory of a once, a faraway love.
Then up from wiry, dense root-pods
a woman formed before me.
Her hair—shadows on the mountain at dusk.
Her chin—a rock
the final stone to seal my den.

II.

The den caved in. I cooked over
coals—the dust of my home. Burnt up.
Frizzled. In every crevice there is
more hunger once the first hunger
is acknowledged. And I'm guilty,
guilty for everything.
How could this house collapse?
How could this woman turn to dust?
"All illusion," books will whisper.
Nothing could be better than this.

III.

There's a river where entire villages
thrive—once both erect and soft.
The time in which I've taken this body
is flat time—running long and drying up.
A voice continues to question me: "Could you
ever be self-defined?" I say yes. But some
words were not handed to me because I asked

for them. Some memories, some rods
and hooks will pierce me, love, even as you
reach for me so tenderly now.

MY MOTHER THE ROSARY BEAD

after Laura Kasischke

And Encanto hopscotch. And a nervous stomach. And Our Lady of the Sacred Heart locked in the pews. The Navy children of the Quonsent hut. My mother running calloused fingers across a prayer book. While her rosary, the Desperate Morning Hour, adorns the breasts of barn owls. While her rosary, the Desperate Morning Hour, gleams off Alsatian glass. While her rosary, the Desperate Morning Hour, forms the pearls of sweat on the clavicles of demons.

WHAT'S A GOD HOLE?

in response to my mom's suggestion that what's wrong with human beings is they all have God holes

Is it a pinprick? Just need
  a dab of cotton, even the shirt
  you're wearing.

Or is it a gash? Definitely
  requiring water, bandages
  for a few hours.

Is it more of a strawberry? Burns
  for a minute, looks bad, very scabby,
  quick to dry.

Or is it a deep, deep wound? We're talking hospital
  style. Alcohol, gauze, sutures, antibiotic
  drip, the whole bit. These holes
  don't close up quickly
  reopen easily
  definitely leave a scar
  the kind you show your friends

  or hide.

HISTAMINE

I think a ghostly hand lives in my home,
throws shards of peppercorn into my eyes.
I also think this ghostly hand had kids
inside my tissue box, my comforter.
They feed on mango, raisins, cantaloupe,
banana pie, pecan. They sleep in down.
The germination of my throat complete,
their knuckles choose my skull to knead.

My father met a priest who cures disease
who ties reactions and attacks to past
ancestral pangs, conducts a healing mass
for those affected. Earth records abuse—
blood fertilizing soil, ocean-soaked
canyons carved out of bones. He blesses sites
of death and grief. I wonder if I had
a great great grandfather who beat his wives,
his children, and although they've died by now,
their fingers pollinate my chest, my head
because they're out to get what's left of him.

My lover rings, but I don't hear the phone
over the breasts of women being sliced.
A young boy tugs his father's shirt for love.
His index finger presses a rifle's tongue.
My whispered name evaporates inside
the muffled consternation of small ghosts
and my own fingers scratching at my eyes.

SNAFU

It's actually an acronym   SNAFU

Situation
Normal
All
Fucked
Up

Crass really. If my parents knew
and I guess they should have
they wouldn't have used it: SNAFU.

Much like *suck* but angrier
for which my brother and I were berated
in an art store, middle-America.

The fact of this ignorance
embarrasses me much like the Trivial Pursuit
game I played with cinema coworkers on down time

when I couldn't conjure Stalin's name
in the history pie. I cried in Theatre 3,
the smallest one.

Even now I don't trust I got it right.
My memory as receding as the lover's hairline
I so hoped to wander forever. SNAFU.

It's about war. It's not about
losing a screw or getting sick
on the way to the train. I want

to know everything. I want to respect
the dead, to not be wrong. Most of my life
I had no idea SNAFU stands for something

like chaos theory without the luxury
of pontification. The gas at the gas
station erupts across my thigh. Somebody,

light a match.

HYMN OF THE PROSELYTE

> *Then I went down to the walnut grove / to see the new green by the brook, / to see if the vine had budded, / if the pomegranate trees were in flower.*
> —The Song of Songs

A pious girl
waving her arms
at charismatic conventions

An earnest lector
proclaiming
This is the Word of the Lord

In folk choir
cantillating
Hail Mary Gentle Woman

The host dissolving
on a faithful tongue
a solemn *Amen*

There is nothing
wrong with Jesus
but the God of childhood
is inextricably tied
to parental
perspective
to what is human

and an emerging woman
will likely cut
her mainspring loose
under the weight
of scrutiny
or abuse

Old enough to return
to a compassionate
creator
long forgotten
perhaps never before
known

It takes this new Name
to open river
again into sea

~

Floating for decades
an uprooted western sycamore
in the often unnoticed
San Diego River
catches occasional scrub
on the shoreline
remains supine

mottled bark drenched
splitting as it matures

an irregularly branched crown
its trunk and arms
assuming many shapes

Fire blight crossed
in cultivation
a hybrid plane tree

broad leaves borne
alternately on the stem

~

Turning corners
the Torah shakes

its letters
at once a caress
at once a stinger
of the bee that is religion
and I want it
but look at me
bending at the knee
singing the Sh'ma
a Catholic girl
of an Apostles'
Creed all
the sacraments
I gave up those
Our Fathers
and here they are again
Adonais pushed out
my mouth like jacaranda
suddenly blooming mid
May in San Diego
Modah Ani upon rising
and I am grateful beseeching
Was I born to utter *Lord*
Can I help I like to pray

A SPARROW IN MY FIREPLACE

She, so brown, I can barely distinguish
her from the dusted brick. She scoots
under a wrought iron grate where oak blocks warmed
and left us only ash.
The sparrow panics and seizes against the frame
filling the house
with the sound of wings pressing on air.
She opens her narrow beak to breathe.

I'll wait for you to come home and bury her
in a Kleenex box full of dried aster.
My fingers brush skin into vane.
The floors move wooden plumage. The washrag pushes
wings across the counter.
After she is stiff in your palms
will you touch me like a terrified finch?
Your heart pushing on a feathered throat,
your hands timid, your lips like a trembling beak?

I dream a convention of birds
where thrush breath cools my skin
and painted buntings play in my hair.
When mourning doves peck for gravel, they vibrate
the ground where we set in the front yard
puffing out our chests and singing out of rusty throats.
In my dream, the young bird does not die
because I was afraid to release her.

PLEASE PRAY

Please pray for the woman at the piano in a hotel
lobby, her arthritic hands poised for silence

Please pray for the couples who thrust into gym equipment
to avoid stepping inside other strangers

Please pray for the babies of the wedded ones
who offer them an excuse to sleep in separate beds

Please pray for the widowed postal employee
waiting for word in the oncology ward

Please pray for the drunken man found
face down in the condo courtyard fountain

Please pray for the young girl
who discovered him while looking for her Dora

Please pray for Dora, the idol,
the scapegoat, the icon, the future

TRANSFERRED IN TEXAS

Sometimes a phone call
or a bowl of soup or
a billboard from God
is all you need to be
high & easy again.
I prefer everything
that's Flying J—the shower,
the hot water, the
public computer keyboard.
Reading sweetness. Some
strange sights to be seen
if you look—the window
display at the Columbus
Exterminating Company
that makes art of murder,
the truckstop employee
standing before me
who puts his hand up,
says hello, asks,
—How are you?
—Good. You?
—Good. You're lookin' good.
—Thanks.
—I'm Robby.
—Heather. Temporarily unavailable.
I don't think he knew
I was referring
to the Road Link Server.
—Hey, you drive a truck?
—Nah. Just cars.
But that's something,
isn't it?
—Honey,
that's good enough for me.

GARNISH

The diner waitress garnishes
the plate edge with chive specks,
a chaotic circle of green,
so that any bite
we pull toward ourselves
will subtly bite us back.
She's a professional.

I myself have tried
to make what I serve
more tempting—a dash
of paprika on the latke,
cinnamon teasing the challah,
olives serving as a gate
to and from the hummus.

We do what we can
to have a little more
beauty.

Outside, a gardener stuffs
a lavender stem
into her pocket, tucks
a wildflower behind her ear.
The creditors, after her
for loans she cannot pay,
choose the last emptying,
the garnishment of the wage.

To embellish.
To impoverish.

It is something like
the boy on steroids
gaining muscle but

losing potency,
the aging forehead
treated with botox
to decrease wrinkles
to no longer crease
when indicating empathy.

The homeless man
swoops in on the untouched
melon rinds in those few seconds
between the sated guests'
departure and
the bussing of waste.

A waste that depletes
sustains.

THE SEDUCTION OF OBJECTS

The books I've been reading
line up like chorus girls
suspended in a position
I unconsciously choreographed
and then watched
live in my borrowed living room.
If we chose to believe, we could be
seduced by anything.
We'd look around our present spaces—
at the tacky movie poster bracing itself
against the drywall as though enjoying
the pain of being taken by surprise.
Who's the next love victim?
The globe crouching in the corner
anxious to be turned, tired
of only one side showing?
Or the dusty albums lilting to the right,
resting their weight upon each other
sleepy, safe and singing?
Even the TV antennae taunt me
with two fingers gesturing me
to come closer. Think of the coasters,
videotapes, cushions, picture
frames we could manhandle.
I will hold each flirtatious thing
and in declaration
of my love decry:
I'm going to touch you now
my red wooden alarm clock.
Chipped ceramic vase, you are open
to be kissed. Or am I so in love with motion
that I assume these plastics,
porcelains and cottons desire
to be enlivened? Perhaps, if given
the choice, the records would remain

in numb, stacked symmetry.
The antennae wouldn't care to reach
for anybody. And the world
still proven round
would contentedly nestle, stationary,
unmoved by the idea of something so fragile
spinning out of control.

NAKED AT THE JAZZ

The woman in the painting and the man
she's teasing have a fig between them
open, halved. She will let him
penetrate her from behind
later but for now it's cosmos
and the bodies becoming other bodies.
Yes, I know it's the table but I'm telling
you it's a fig.

FRONTAGE

I have loved the crumbling facade of Maurizio Carni
in the bastard piazza better than any one-stop sprawl
of the Walmarts of America

its letters as aggressive as beef
its beats the song of alert flesh.

On the terraza across I order a peroni not even noon
try to hide my photographing exploitation of the moment
behind a red napkin box and a glass ashtray.

Storefronts announcing particularity:
My name is Maurizio.
I sell meat.

LONELY PLANET TRAVEL GUIDES

Last night I slept with Mexico.
He was sitting there, above the blanket,
a little cold on the outside
before I invited him in
and he got under the covers
of my daily bed.

He was showing me
Chihuahua, his skin heating up
as I folded him back at the corners
of his shoulders while he drove
me from dry and long
to southerly.

I won't say much about the borders
except for the smoky laughing
on Revolución.
Somewhere between there and Jalisco
he had had his way with me. I started
warming up, wearing him down
with my fingers, fevered
on his shape.

And when we crossed over
into landscape unfamiliar,
I had begun if ever
so slightly to discover
the tackle of his capital,
the color of his conquest.

Have you met the highlands of Chiapas?
Howler monkeys scream
from distant kilometers. I was even convinced
I wanted to join them, but for him,
calling me up the road to San Cristóbal.

As I rose up the mist and cold again,
we came to the end, he and I,
at the top where the cage around the chest shudders
and bursts open.

AN ANTI-LONGING POEM

never rides in couplets. It makes you
feel like shit and like it.
No epiphanies, no pensive pauses.
Sharp harsh consonants. And rhyme
sins each time. No we's, no you's. No
pretty alliteration. An anti-longing poem doesn't
care that he got uncomfortable you didn't pull
your leg away when it brushed his. *You sick pig.*
An anti-longing poem doesn't glorify his gigantic
eyes—the more specialized the more
exaggerated the mammal.
An anti-longing poem doesn't rest on the "Sortie"
sign and wonder how its ending
is pronounced or try to make meaning
of the variations and failures with language.
An anti-longing poem doesn't contemplate
failure. An anti-longing poem never fails.
It describes the bitters on the bar
from a safe distance, objectivity
her saddlebag. The drunk at 56 degrees struggling
to finish his pitcher holds no glamor, no golden
weight. He is simply a man ingesting Boreal Rousse
wishing he had ordered a Cocombre Ton. No, there are no
wishes in anti-longing poems.

In an anti-longing poem I wouldn't
fellate every semi-conscious being in the bar.
I wouldn't interpret their smirks for desire.
I wouldn't believe I were wantable
somehow more luminous in oil light and cheap
wood countertops but gente I am human
and I will always want more than I have
play the role of object to a subject
imagine a stranger in white tee wants to caress me.
I will drink too much and obsess over the last

slurp of Boreal Blonde. I will long and long
and long and somebody will want to read
about it and somebody won't

and I don't blame them.

I BLAME YOU, HENRY DAVID THOREAU

I went to the woods because I wished to live deliberately…and not, when I came to die, discover that I had not lived.

I blame you, Henry David Thoreau,
for emboldening me, for making me
believe I must, like Horace,
seize the fucking day.
You know what's
happened
every time I've seized?

I've been
ignored
mocked
rejected
in the full glory of scabby knees.

I've been alone thanks to your
hypocritical solitary concoction

or did I misunderstand?
Did you mean seize the rail
the fishing pole
the car keys

not the desire
for the beautiful stranger
not the paper
on which only a fool
would compose
such desperate, impotent pleas?

I blame Walt Whitman, too,
but that's a different asshole.

HOW TO GET RID OF HICKEYS

This is the caliber of article I now scour.

What gets me here?

I type the following
yes of course into Google:

"how get over ex new girlfriend"

or

"break up recover when"

that sort of thing.

The blogs, ezines, dot-com grammar and mechanics
are awful—
misuse of there/their/they're
absolutely no apostrophe
awareness.

Absolutely no credibility.

But I read on.

Link after
Link
after...

You get the picture.

Until
a small
peace
emerges
from

this

degradation

until

the night
comes
when
I
really
will

need to read

How to Get Rid of Hickeys.

GETTING OFF

That's how they'll find me—
shucked over the edge
of the bed, underwear around
my ankles
some rubbing object below me—
snuffed out during a final attempt
at pleasure and release.

I wonder who'll tell or what
the story will be: she died
in her sleep, cardiac arrest
while doing pushups, cause of death
unknown. They can't say I didn't try.
What else can one do all alone
but wonder of what
the body is capable?

For my friends who secretly know the cause
of my death, the hardest search will be
for the answer to this question: had she at least
gotten off before she left this world?
Will they postulate my last sensation
and the scenario of my final fantasy?
They'll hope I was imagining something
extraordinary and not envisioning
a cucumber or some
submissive violation scene.
Let me have been in Canyon de Chelly,
Niagara Falls, or some other landmark
being pleasured by all the lovers
who ever shunned me.
Or let me have been communing
with God, so transcendent as to no
longer need another human body
to fulfill me.

What's it like to die
in the middle of an orgasm
like those self-strangulators
found in their closets,
those private thrill-seekers
bottles placed
where bottles weren't meant to be?
I wonder if there's a separate heaven
for people who kick the bucket
in an ecstatic state perpetually appeasing
unsatisfied angels.

Or did I never reach climax
and so, will haunt hookers
and harems in international
bedrooms eternally spread open
enslaved by a body
I'll no longer be encased in?

Is desire finite? Let desire be finite.
Give my family and other loved
ones peace so that they might
sigh and say, at least she's in a place
where she'll never have to pull
her pants down,
try so hard,
or even remember a life
when masturbation was the ultimate
in requisite pastime.

CATEGORIES OF SEX

robe sex
i'm bored sex
can't sleep sex
it's been so long so we probably should sex
you disgust me but i'll let you anyway sex
want it so bad cum in two seconds sex
i'm too drunk sex
you are a new species i want to discover every inch of sex
i'm imagining you're your best friend sex
i'm not sure if you're a man or a woman sex
don't know where your body ends and mine begins sex
woke up and we're having sex sex
not awake enough yet to remember i don't love you anymore sex
i'm pretending to be your mother sex
awkward car sex
cold floor why are we doing it here sex
condom broke my life is ruined sex
oh my god i really can feel pleasure sex
can't we try something different sex
i wish i were trained as a gymnast sex
sore for ten days after sex
i think we took it too far sex
the dog is looking at us funny sex
we're having so much sex we're not even eating sex
uncontrollable tears sex
roll over with my back to you sex
bring me to climax without even touching me sex
i'm convinced we're in the ocean sex
this can't be human sex
somebody might call the cops sex
tender sex
we got a little rough let's not talk about it sex
yoga certification sex
not even one song was over yet sex
i'd rather be masturbating sex

mediocre desperate stranger sex
i wish i felt something sex
selfish sex
same old fantasy sex
i hope you're too tired to go through with it sex
let's just stop it's not happening tonight sex
we're the two sexiest creatures on the planet sex
hungry sex
lazy sex
angry sex
did i turn off the stove sex
god i've gotten fat sex
were you always this hairy sex
our bodies were created for one another sex
fuck we're out of condoms sex
nervous fumbling sex
this means more to you than it does to me sex
stop sweating on me sex
why did i come over sex
i know it's over sex
are you comparing me to your ex sex
i just made a noise i've never heard before sex
your eyes have gone hollow sex
i have no idea how our bodies just did that sex
doing everything we can without actually having sex sex
i wish i never started this sex
you can do anything you want to me sex
frustrated phone sex
railway car vestibule sex
filthy club bathroom sex
still smell you on the drive to work sex
all night long and I want you more sex
i see where this is going
sex

FLOWERING-TIME RESPONSE: ON CHANGING WALDEN POND'S FLOWERS

> *The plants that are declining seem to be the plant families that can't change their blooming times in response to changing temperatures.*

Her arms the petals of dogwood in pondwater   pirouette
past the deer ticks
past the biologist and her subjects investigating minnows
past the daily sunbathers sucking sun with the addiction of baby bird
    to a mother's crop
past the beloved's indifferent goodbye
past the work it takes to stay alive
past the sunset of fertility
past the swimmer's frantic laps
past the man's narrow frame the branding of his body on her desire
past desire
spinning swirling only breeze and current turning the blossoms
under Concord maple
under persecutioners' pines

THE BOAT NEXT TO ILLUSION

is for sale.

Perks:
Your western neighbor
calls himself Tabasco Cat
and this eastern rubble
prefers anonymity

unless you seek a naming
to which of course you are
entitled.

The boat next to Illusion
is for sale.

Recommendations:
Avoid peeking into her frosty
windows.
Steer clear of her
late night unguided tours.
Don't talk to her captain.

And you will ride easy
as you watch seasalt
and marine layer
S
I
N
K

Y
O
U

Price: Negotiable

THE BLUE LINE

Riding the T from Revere
on the blue line, the longest line

blue Beachmont, blue Orient Heights, blue Aquarium,
blue Maverick

green and red move quickly
no line endures like the blue line

on the blue line
motley bodies dunk in ocean, softserve & Bill Ash's Lounge

on the blue line
a drunk not even forty shouts, "Spics, chinks, what are you lookin' at?"

on the blue line pedicures chip, women hide belly fat,
boys readjust sweaty Red Sox caps

on the blue line
Cohen whispers, *Dance me to the end of love.*

alone or coupled, either way,
it's the blue line

Sam Turin's lungs collapsed last night,
morphine drenched, and Daniel recited the Sh'ma

blue blue blue blue line, flatline,
blue Wood Island, blue State, blue Wonderland, blue Suffolk Downs

VALLEY OF THE SHADOW

for Noah

I walk in the dark valley that gives me courage.

Driving the dark road through pines, two-lanes Appalachia
closes in on me, the dense midday lack of light.
But, it expands too, opening up the hills like I'd lifted
a basement double door or a floodgate and watched
the breadth of it come alive
like a worm.

Jimmie Rogers crying and yodeling, dark about a sweetheart,
once, and all kinds of stories about people with names.
Appalachia, your sweet leaves fill root beds, dust themselves
by piling up—breathe even in suffocation.
I inhale you as I pull over, delirious from not eating, lost
in curves that scare the truckers, force them to swear
"I'm never comin' back this way again." They roll
in the permanent whine of brake pads, rotors starting to grind.
Damp yellow scent of mulch, you draw me into the shear canyon.
Call me to feel my body monkeybar down branches
knotted in their own archways.

Light hardly passes through to this road where I've pulled over.
Frantically in the shell, I shove crackers into my mouth
like a welder fusing empty space.
I gulp cranberry juice from the cooler.

I could fear no evil.

When the rigs have tweaked into another maze—turns
out of audible distance—I am left with the leaves
and the desire to jump, laughing out of physical deprivation
into more pleasure from somersaulting through pines. I'm alert
roadside. Almost instantly my blood sugars. Two wood doors
close. I lie in the thick dust and let the cool drift over me.
My skin for the first time feeling absolute shade.

CALIFORNIA POPPY

I drove the back roads of my hometown, listening to Mexican corridos, having gone these ways many times before unnoticing of the emerging orange until, out of ordinary grass, I discovered a poppy.

As people, now utterly earth-bound, will probably always see the ocean of our history, I couldn't help but believe the plant's body grew sea-green and budded anemones. The neon blossoms sheltered the sea spider inside which held together the stem and the flower, amphibiously petaled. Out of ordinary grass, how can a thing be so bold as the fish that glows in the dark of the ocean floor?

I didn't know what else to do but remove my camera from its case and take black and white pictures of the spring that startled me. The music had turned to commercials by the time I started the car, and grass became ordinary again, and the roads became too windy for me to notice in color radiant, temporary beauty.

DEVELOPING PHOTOGRAPHS

Behind the life of my mouth is a photograph
of Mary, the Virgin, when she was alive.
When she took me to the railcar
of my own pilgrimage to Lourdes.
The first night was Orleans
where I slept with Joan of Arc in the rain.
The drops from her statued sword
nestled between my lips and to fill my canteen.

What's more important: an image or the taste?
What's captured in the slow exposure of time?
I don't sleep on trains.
I may miss a grapevine
or a figure hidden in the boards
of an ivy shack.
Always moving—the eyes must open.

I think Joan of Arc lost her innocence in battle
when her people no longer trusted her,
when they removed their faith
and replaced it with desire.

On the tracks slowing down
for the ghost bodies—the latent
images of saints—they wait
in transparent skirts, cloudy blue
wind of the machine.
And on their knees, the penitents
crawl forward to Guadalupe.

There is a picture of Claire in Assissi
as phantomed as the inside of a candle.
Her profile in a dark, tiny chapel

is what reminds me of light.

Dear Scabbed Unrecovered Visionaries

Our faces are hidden from one another.
We move and blur. We spin
out of recognition
and what's left to be seen is
all we've made or done.

The photographs on our tongues.

PACIFIC

for you whose deaths I will carry

Did you die because I taught you to swim at night
when the air was too dry to stay outside of water?
Was the last living thing to see you
a sea duck diving for fish?
blue-footed booby
harlequin duck
tricolored heron
Whom have you seen?

August air doesn't move
since I've migrated east.
Heat curls a photograph I saved
taken the day of your flat top—
all curlicues gone. The barber shop
rocked on an auburn ocean.
Surfbird, dad cried into mom's silence.
Your head swooped like the decurved bill
of a white-faced ibis.
I supported the cut though I grew,
little sister, with your hair in my hands.

Refusing scissors I pulled tangles
looped up near your scalp, bubble gum,
rubberbands not made for human hair,
clumps of sand I'd have to wet to shake loose.

I watched sweat slide from your neck
that hairless season. I watched
sand stick to your salty, wide-open forehead.
I begged to rub your skull
shining in my eyeglasses.

Three years ago, I avoided the mourners
filling themselves with salmonballs and quiche.

This August, I ignore the sweat
running down my own hairline
matting a colorless bob.
I cover my head in bandanas, umbrellas,
a wig, a paper scrap, tablecloths,
a lack of light, a book,
canvas, cotton, straw.
I close my pores at the sink
but your curls are still threaded
somewhere between my fingernails and our hairbrush.

Hair is dead skin kept alive with care.
Your hair.
What I held onto was dead.
You left my hands floating in water.
Dizzy in heat I watch for your arrival
through the toss of the ceiling fan
and the crossbreeze,
in the rustle of thorn scrub and mesquite,
as nightfall in the pit of summer.

I am land sacked
with sage thrashers and cactus wrens
a very large wren of arid country. White stripe over eye
and white spots in outer tail...Voice: a monotonous chuh-chuh;
chuh-chuh, etc., or chug-chug-chug-chug, on one pitch gaining
rapidity; unbird-like

44 EAST

Missouri
        a lighter green
                that swells
in wind
bugs nearly louder than
                Mack trucks
generating
                cool sleep
for drivers a lot like me
        taking care of the soul
        this is messy
                business
this takes a lot of friendship
and the search for love
        that's one task
                measure
                the worth of it
and see what you
come up with
        next time you're in
                Illinois
look for me

A TOWN IN MASSACHUSSETTS

for my friends

Standing in the Berkshires
envisioning a Green River
and a blanket laid out like a world
we lay out in fatter moons
and the language
of dreaming.

Where I will wait up until I hear
the owls. Now it's cicadas
and women sleeping
loving each other even in sleep.
Where you are making a kind
of life.

Here we commune in a meekness
a sweetness that allows us
to open up notebooks, songbooks,
goofy looks and be judged only
by a creator so fine as to have made
these trees—the ones
not yet lost.

When I wake up I might
have a story on my tongue.
I might mimic your style and sing.
By then you'll have found
another home within
a radius unknown to you yet
and I'm pretty sure you'll be in
my story
                    even then.

Steps leading to a recreated
barn—all our homes

are our creations. A legacy?
Is that the ones we've loved?
Is my story forever told
in the skin of the ones to come?
Or do I stop when she stops?
Do I move when he moves on?

Some have traveled
to cabins in other woods
and we retreat to our notebooks,
songbooks, the looks of
the unjudged, the romantics who can
come up with a reason
for not yet ending.

MIND THE FROGS

I.

Eggs in a makeshift pond—
a pool on the perimeter of my childhood
home when it rained more in Ramona.
I was a girl perplexed by the lives of frogs.
These wiggly-headed larvae with gills,
metamorphosing. Basin one day empty, the next
teeming with polliwogs. The best jumpers
of the vertebrates. Where do they
come from? Tails resorbed into legs.
The call, alone and in chorus, for a mate
back to water, often the same water
bodies in which they were born.
Breathing through their skin,
secreting poison. Three-chambered hearts.

II.

Frogs roam the staircases of Guanajuato. Sliding toward hidden doors,
they giggle at hostelers like me seeking budget lodging
in already impoverished places.
And Don Quixote still gets the spot in the window at El Secreto
de la Lluvia, a cafe for vino tinto and Dolores' postres.

Down in the plaza, literature students venerate the conquistador,
initiate the Cervantes festival. I must admit, I bought a postcard.
Spanish class textbooks enforce a Castillian *vos* we won't use, no need
for the familiar plural you. When the you becomes plural, don't
trust it.

Tourists to Chiapas labor over the rolled 'r', gasp and slobber, "It's so
cheap here in San Cristóbal," then haggle over two-dollar
handwoven rebosos that took three days to make.

Señor Frog's in Ensenada does great business for springbreakers
in sombreros guzzling pitchers of margaritas, *dos por uno*. Girls
from Oaxaca bought and sold north here, too.

Gullies, tunnels, deserts and El Rio Grande. An occasional cross.
Bottles of water exorcised by Minutemen. The border aches
with loss.
La/El Mexican@ hones the art of amphibiousness. Mind the frogs
in the fire escapes, luminous roaming leaves.

III.

A final recognition of goodbye offers the greatest reward.
The head nod. The lift of the hand in a public place.
That was our finale, a mutual misunderstanding.
Vacancy consumed your face. Let it pass

like all the others in these city squares—Brattle,
Rotonda, Red—let our words babble
as the babies' in the strollers whining by.
Let them dislodge. Let there be no trace.

We can leave our kisses in the subway
station, a restaurant, parking spaces,
somewhere between land and water
feed what we've been
to the amphibians.

Some beautiful toad dines tonight,
good meal, can't quite pinpoint the taste.
Some beautiful toad imbibes
and like confusion
eventually
is gone.

PERSIMMONS

I trace the seasons
this way, by this orchard,

where Traylor and Highland
converge, amid grassland,

where wildlife research
has won against gated developments.

My hometown offers plenty
of questionable pursuits:

nationalism, rodeos,
family values, methamphetamine.

But the grove line
redeems this place.

In fall, still grieving
love lost, I pay for a bucket

to fill with red-orange harvest.
One after the other, I pluck

alone, under a sky of their ripe
heavy tart sweet—strange

to most Americans
while I greedily add

more to my pail
already overflowing.

Then winter
which seems never

to end. Bare branches
only crows desire.

Spare, gray
reminding the living

there will always be
the dead. Now,

spring I sometimes resent
its joy, its perkiness,

its refusal to stop coloring.
And at first I am not moved

by the jade leaves.
Where is the fruit in these?

But I look closer. And nestled
deep in the green

the birth
the very core

opens, opening
ever so slowly

opening star
of persimmon.

ALONG THE SAN JOAQUIN

If possible, postpone your trip until the fog lifts, usually by late morning.

In the midnight tule fog
of California's Central Valley
where agriculture thrives
and pesticides silently infect,
I deliver on a deadline,
clambering Interstate 5.
Protected by an assembly
of parts—steel skin, internal
combustion—I fear I may not
survive this highway miasma,
known to cause the most weather
related casualties in the state.
But I am discerning
direction by a sudden
singular semi
in the slow lane
inches away
and tremulous too.
I must trust
this living thing before me,
a ballast incarnate—
its cautious speed,
its tail lights,
a halo of red.

BLUE PETER

a blue flag with a white square in the center, flown at the head of the foremast of a vessel about to leave port

At the center of my sorrow
there resurrected a lighthouse.
A few creaky rooms spiraled
toward the lamp,
surrounded in the blues.
I found a staircase
the banister of which
I had to grasp tightly
and my body required
the posture of a crouched animal.
Then the final stretch
presented a ladder to me
wrought iron, perfect vertical.
Ascent commanded a climber's strength
utilizing shoulders, forearms,
quadricepital grace.
At the top I discovered the lantern—
much larger than I expected
yet seemingly insignificant
when compared to the sea
though the eyes of mariners watch for it
like apocalypse.
The flag I wear at the face
of my vessel neither
warns nor directs. It announces
its intent to move, both
reminds itself and tells the others
I am bound in blue circumscription
and at the pivot
a lightbox will reveal
my faithful story.

Acknowledgments

Thank you to all the family members, teachers, friends, colleagues, and strangers who have contributed to my confidence and inspiration. You remain partly to blame for why I wield words in the form of poetry. Thank you to my parents, Carlene and Ken Eudy; to Blake, Kim, and Paige; and to my late grandparents, especially Isabelle Mars, to whom I promised I'd one day publish my work. Thank you to my teachers and guides: Sandra Alcosser, Rabbi Lenore Bohm, Phyllis Burke, Marilyn Chin, Glover Davis, Linda Holler, David Matlin, Patricia Mihalik, Cecile Pineda, and Ramona Szczerba. Thank you to the beloveds and cherished friends who have helped shape me into the woman I am and supported the poet in me in countless ways: Marie Alfonsi, Olga Alicea, Kelly Harmon Durant, Carlos Fernandez, Debbie Fix, Noah Gallagher, Sanam Govari, Lisa Jones, Daniel Krupitski, Michelle Lenoue, Tanya McCrory, Trissy McGhee, Kris Olmsted, and Susan Tidey. Thank you to Kia Bowman for the blessing of the life you lived with boldness and artistry. Thank you to Hector Martinez and Lauren Mason, poet comrades of my MFA years. Thank you to the Montreal Summer Literary Seminars poets: Hadara Bar-Nadav, Tony Hoagland, Sierra Nelson, Nat Sufrin, and Binoy Zuzarte. Thank you to Nancy Cary, Kelly Mayhew, Jim Miller, and all who contribute to the success of San Diego City Works Press. Thank you to Andy Peck and Roni Silver for your support and generosity. And finally, thank you to the three incredible poets and human beings I have the privilege to work with and nestle near in this book and in San Diego daily life: Chris Baron, Cali Linfor, and Sabrina Youmans. Your faith, humor, and companionship have given me the courage to attach my name to these dotted lines.

Notes

"Getting Chastised by John Lee Hooker" italicized portions come from the lyrics of "It Serves You Right to Suffer" by John Lee Hooker.

"Post-Nicotrol" was published, in a slightly different form, in *Hunger and Thirst*, City Works Press, 2008.

"Hymn of the Proselyte" epigraph comes from *The Song of Songs* translated by Chana Bloch and Ariel Bloch.

"An Anti-Longing Poem" is dedicated to Sierra Nelson.

"I Blame You, Henry David Thoreau" epigraph comes from *Walden*.

"Flowering-Time Response" epigraph comes from an October 2008 NPR.org article entitled "Climate Changing Walden Pond's Flowers."

"Valley of the Shadow" title and italicized portions comment on Psalm 23 of *The Bible*.

"California Poppy" is forthcoming, in a slightly different form, in *The Far East Magazine*, So Say We All, 2012.

"Pacific" final italicized lines come from *Peterson: A Field Guide to Western Birds*.

"Persimmons" is forthcoming, in a slightly different form, in *The Far East Magazine*, So Say We All, 2012.

"Along the San Joaquin" epigraph comes from www.wrh.noaa.gov.

"Blue Peter" epigraph is a dictionary entry.

A Book of Ugly Things

Cali Linfor

Contents

LYRIC IN THE LIGHT

Body, remember.
—C.P. Cavafy and Kenny Fries

Poets play the lyre. Sound-Chest,
the resonator, muscle
memory. The cavity,
hollow that never empties.

Burial of grief behind lung,
near the heart's inferior
vena cava. Shiva's stomp.
Mourning in both breath and blood.

Shame sisters with rage, a twitch
of the eye. Helpless, hopeless
the bowel contracts, panics, bolts.
Terror, a void, in the mouth.

The psychologists now know
this is back of the brain stuff—
Abreaction. Autonomic
arousal. Somatic dreaming.

Closed throat, shut eye, mute, deaf, blind.
Too much for time to hold still.
We cannot write it down yet.
Our body does, tissue thin.

We need. We want. We call out.

A naming ceremony,
for moments without sanction.
Fill the place, Word-Song. We are
tongued again. Trebled and based.

Hang the lamps too in bare trees.
True, winter is harsh, stealing

the leaves, sun so far away,
but this makes the light brighter.

The lantern tree is also
a lyric. Not a lament.
There is room for both keening
sorrow and singable joy.

MATILIJA POPPY

Near the warning that if you speed,
a child that cannot hear you might die,
blooms the egg poppy, overblown.
The ovum of a bird cracked open by the sky.

The yard to my right is a horror
of twisted evergreen, limp palms, and snake holes.
Yellow spotted even in spring,
the work of a spider's dews and dapples.

Who dies inside? What poverty
of time and care allows the weeds to grow?
Who is too old and so alone that no one offers?
Not even a neighbor out of borrowed shame.

Our yard, never pretty, is wretched
with foxtail, a knee-high float encouraged
by a wet winter and pneumonia
dampening our lungs and home.

We have no labor in us.

Matilija poppy, glabrous, perennial, branched,
woody at the base, shrubby, grows eight feet tall
and needs no tending. A native showgirl
I have tried to coax into my garden.

She attends where she will. She is ugly too
but so full of pollen and glitz, we don't see it.
She perceives the shadow behind the window
and seeds herself here.

THE SETTING

We pull up in our Chevy, step out,
and don't even bother to lock the doors.
Everything is still here: the stucco apartment,
dipping pepper trees, honeysuckle bush,
Kawa's Market, and the empty lot.

Half-moon tires, mustard grass,
and Camaro bones litter the east side.
The west side is brailled with bike tracks
retained in mud, and in the back
an old plywood fort leans into itself.

Just north lies the bramble where they found me.
Ladybug, three-leaf clover, mint, daffodil,
foxtail, and snail have all grown over
the holes my heels dug out.

A belt buckle's crescent rise, grass scrapes,
and a five-fingered bruise swelled my right side.
My left side was purple-blue, painted
by boot heel and toe. In my back
stretched the perfect circle of a knee.

It is not enough for you to just listen
for pastel shotgun houses, shell-rock alleys,
and the hot dust behind a caboose. I kick stray cans
until you decide it's time to climb into the car
and drive fifty miles home.

The first time you touched me, I trembled. Passion, yes,
but something else, something involuntary. I closed up
so tight no man could get in. You had to know why
and who. I only know the place.

When bedtime comes, I'll pitch over you like a tent.
I'll block the moon's light and whisper. Read my body.

Trace the scar initialing my breast, suck the pockmark
of a cigarette from my ear, and hear the ladybug
caught in my throat. Go ahead, dig
your hands and tongue into me.

WAIL

Fear, I release you.
—Joy Harjo

Where there is water, in the west, there is La Llorona.
I live in a cemented city, so she banshees my sewer
among the baseballs, dead leaves, trickle of wet, rats, and possums.
A woman veiled in sorrow. I am grown so she does not want me
anymore. She collects only children. Her wretched and greedy grief
make the wind wail in the night. She scares me differently now.
Moonlit, even a storm's slim puddle will cast a mirror, house us together.

The snot and splotch
the open mouth
letting the sound out
in an achy ribbon.

We stutter the cry.

Our hands clutch
and shake, tear
at the hair,
form a fist
for the mouth
that will not shut.

We bite down.

Our bellies float and twist
in a carnival of trembling.

Eventually, a cloud will drift the moon dark, turn the water
into water again, release this mad address of misery—the wild eyes,
free me from the boney reach. The unrippled surface will glint empty.

But the fear lingers and I am alone with it squared in my chest.

I carry it around with me,
in the day, far away
from any water,
this childhood terror.

I don't even know
it is there
until I touch it
and feel
how old it is,
how fruitful,
how hidden.

Like a carpenter bee,
it teethes my esophagus
and slips down again
like sap burning
my shoulder blades,
my spine,
making my heartbeat
sticky.

In another city, further south with more water, I rock my child back into slumber when he awakes frightened from dreaming of zombies and golems, fearing around the corner and under the bed. I tell him every culture makes monsters. Parents, all over the world, want children to obey. Story and flesh are not the same. Sometimes, he cries out because he remembers pain. Children possess a sudden violence. The hard pinch of tiny fingers. A caterpillar admired then crushed for peeing on the hand. They throw rocks, break glass, drown in rivers. A lack of malice makes it better but it hurts. It all hurts.

APOCALYPSE

Happy-go-lucky, let your lives
disheveled run.
—Paul Verlaine

1.
I am under that desk again waiting,
with my neck dutifully covered
by the web of my fingers,
for the bomb to drop.

We have just watched a film
in science class. We know
this will not work.

2.
This dull grey sparrow will make it,
transform into a new species,
and of course, the roaches
can take the heat and lack.
But all the predators,
including us, will go.

The seas will reclaim us
or deny us. Unpotable.
The earth may shatter.

Even now, we are killing
the coyote, rabbit and skunk.
Not for meat or fur
or even meanness
or because they threaten
our young or food.

We lack forethought.
They crossed a road
we could not build
with all of us in mind.

3.

Jesus bleeds.
He is fit. Trim. Muscular.
Overpowered. I know. He submitted.

His strength was not of the body.
But the painters trace the thigh, the shoulder, the chest
in blood,
in thew.
Muscular power, development, strength, vitality,
sinew.

Somehow the word sinew for me is always,
always Christ's neck trembling,
stretching the moment before he drops his head
and sees as if for the first time
the cross he is nailed to—
Jubilation.

4.

Water drums and millet. Powdered milk for the baby.
Beans: pinto, black, and red. Soak them overnight before cooking.

The storehouse must be rotated. We must not be wasteful.
For a month, once a year, we eat mush.

I know I should not believe
the earth will remain generous,
food plentiful and the rain
sweet and drinkable.

5.

The *Twilight Zone* marathon drones
black and white. TV trays dot the living
room. My family gives thanks.

This episode cloys
the throat, a surprise of tears
when we had just been laughing.

The world empty of birdsong
and battle. A lone man stands
blind before a building of books.

You know this fable. If you wear glasses,
love to read, even if you don't. He must live
without even the paper tongue and touch of others.

While I can, I tuck myself into the corner
of my room, tangle-headed
with library books, buried
in the nave I've indented.

6.
An asteroid rumbles to earth.
A giant in the yawn of stars, larger than Manhattan.
The island, a bead again.

The blue tendon of our sky
will not prevent it
from coming.

A hoax I accept as true. A terror
I let into myself like a lake
into a river.

I come home from a 12-hour shift,
my head an ache, a migraine beating the world red
and dangerous.

Extinction possible. The dinosaurs dead
or transformed into alligator, turtle, bird.

April 1. I have forgotten the *War of the Worlds*.
My lover hands me over. I am engulfed by the news.
Reporters I trust say, "The Asteroid is Coming."

Revelations. We have not been to Costco lately.
We don't have enough water

in our LA apartment. Not that it matters.
The shockwave will dissolve us.

I endure the knowing.

At once, our fate
is the same as the deer
standing on the mountainside,
as twirling girls, as jailed men, as their guards,
and as the ocean which will not hold
the waters of its grief.

I hear only the terror
trapped in the sinews
of our throats
like vomit we can't let go.
The sky stops
and the earth falls in a little.

Oh, god. I believe
you are in every rock,
and what is an asteroid
if not a rock?

You are in me and outside
of me as your star falls
onto all of us

your other fallen stars.

DOING DEATH DROPS

I tied my sweater to the monkey bars.
The double-knot of childhood slipped around
my waist—a cradle for the cherry drop.
I hooked one knee and spun against the ground.
They had to seal my mouth to save my tongue.
My mother lost the baby that same day.
She curled inside the puddle of her thighs
and slept to dream the drip of death away.
Our clothes were burned because the blood had dried
before they found us. How could they forget
to wash our hair? She combed the blood from me
and burned the comb. We never speak of it.

THE PASSAGE

When my mother died
so died the passageway

the slice in the earth
from which I emerged.

There could be no returning
to a place more comforting.

We have all seen the place unseen.

IN THE DEEP LINE OF MY LEFT PALM

The x-ray showed a hiccup on the spine. Inside my mother, cancer
pressed like snow against a door and flew like a bee through the ear.
There is no sound quite like it, the throat at a loss, a moan reaching
the teeth, vomit in the sink, the moment before she tells me.

She died pale as a winter morning when starkness is new to the earth,
when sunflowers bury and shades of pink, fruit, and seeds are gone
like a pregnancy fading from the surface of the skin.

Hair spiraling, leaves bathing in a leftover puddle, the dog at the window,
his pressed nose measuring out my grief, wet. I can't believe her last tear
is in the deep line of my left palm.

How do I carry the song of her breath, the dark dream of her eyelash,
cheekbone and throat, this trickle from a luminous eye? I want to call it joy.
Her human salt licking up from an earthy center, hot as laughter, thick as hands
on the back, and as permanent as seeping.

IN BED

My hand curves to your collarbone
as my fingers spread and stretch.

Your nipples peak even before I slide
my thigh around your arching hip.

We barrel roll and I am over you—
ankle laces ankle and calf claims calf.

Breath inside of breath, our chests press until I rise up
to dip down and let my hair dredge the length of you.

I taste open mouth, all my grief at my mother's death
you swallowed, hot and smooth against my teeth.

I taste last Saturday when you rocked me
in your mouth, when you shuddered me.

INSCRIPTION

We like Bukowski because he is from a shithole
and all his words are from a shithole
and only from a shithole—no nightingale
suddenly singing in the midst of all that beer sweat,
car dust, and lonely courageous fucking.

He did have a bluebird
but he kept it in his heart. He held
a singular world in his view.

Repulsion is equal parts attraction.

City poet. The noise and the waste. Fast
food wrappers blown against a stoplight.
It's LA, so no barge is pulling trash
up the river. Some coyote is losing
ground in the desert to our four pounds
a day and the dump, but not
in a Bukowski poem.

He is making money from the cans.

A cat might be killing a bird.
But it's *a* cat and *a* bird. No color.
No names. No setting. Just things
doing what things do.

When we were dating, my husband kept giving me Bukowski.
Very romantic. Every birthday, anniversary, and Christmas.
Three years of books. Prolific. Nothing like a good drunk
to get a man writing. I told him to stop well before we married.

It's not that I didn't like Bukowski
(I would tell my husband)
but I didn't want to own him

even these parts of him printed
on cheap cut paper.

I did not want to make time
for him, for vomit, despair and the lack
of metaphor to give me distance.
I could feel the raised letters, each strike
of his typewriter.

I didn't want him in the room
with me. I didn't want to pack him
into boxes and carry him
every new place I lived.

I read all of them.

Books are a sacrament
sipped between lovers
and I was nineteen and loved
all congress
that is sweet, without hurt,
and well-intentioned.

I did not like them.
They were like soup
to me. The base taste of broth,
what I had to keep my body
going in the hunger of my childhood.

I wouldn't eat it for years.

I gagged at the smell.
It took me a long time
to tell my husband
why I wouldn't
eat soup
and why I didn't want to own
these books.

It doesn't mean I don't own them.
I do. They are inscribed:
To my beloved. I carried
them everywhere.

While I nursed my son,
also for three years,
I ate soup again.
I craved it. Libation.

I eat it still though my milk is well gone
and my breasts are mine again.

Just last week, I read a letter from Bukowski,
followed a link on Facebook, wrote this poem,
thanked him.

THIS BURNING

One

We incinerate
the dead, offer them
up to sky and sea,
let the wind wild,
the cinders cede
what was
in the notion
that nothing
is really left,
or what is left
has rejoined,
seeped in,
reformed.

Grief burns,
light as ash,
stays as a part
of my skin.

Two

There have been so many
memorials for the day
war came again,
flew on wings
we built,
scraped our sky.

We are awash
in lost fathers,
brothers, civilians,
sons and sisters,
fighters of the fire,
mothers, passengers,
pilots, terrorists,
children.

We do not have the hours
to name them all,
so we make time
to mourn. Each loss
doubles the next.

In ceremony,
the violinist holds
sorrow's note, our breath
stilled, tender
to the fingertips.

Then, like smoke
curling from bodies
and buildings, everything
gray and nothing straight,
the bow rises
like a ship
in the far ocean.

Our legs shiver
with the tremble
only grief brings.

The bow possesses
the same shape
that quivers
the arrows.

We weep
because our bodies
melt at a certain heat.

The miracle of floating
on water, the ellipses
of a boat,
holds us above
our certain death.

The bow climbs
the string once more,
saving us too.

Three

To the near dying,
I want to say
I have sat with you,
grandmother,
held your hand,
mother,
washed you, fed you
from my hand,
grandfather,
listened
when you said
you expected to die
in some hobo jungle
and should have,
deserved to, really,
did not sleep,
when you slept
uneasy,
sister,
when you
made no more
song of breath
and no more noise.

I don't grieve the tending,
the catheter, inevitable
bed sore, the slight
heat of the urine bag.

I was loved so I loved.

There is nothing special
in these acts. Tender
though they may be,

they are assured
if we mean to be
human, know life
as mortal, blood,
hair, and bone.

Just as we might attend,
at least once, a birthing.

Use the strength
of us—our voice,
our legs, our hands,
maybe the muscles
of a womb,
to help another
vibrate the air
with that first cry,
perhaps of joy
or shock or something
we can no longer name
that sings, that witnesses.

LIMINAL

A runner spits in the road. Her body damp
as the moment before her lover takes her
in his mouth. One more mile in this heat. One more.

Let the summer go. Let yellow come, then brown.
Birds pant in the sun. Their little tongues undone.
Tiny bellows telling us to take the shade.

But desire is slick. She feels her hips slide then twitch.
Resistance sears the skin, the swallow of breath, the huff
of calf muscle, and the hot tangle of her thighs.

In the time of forest fires, brush can no longer contain itself
and calls forth man to the bush. What mysterious godheat insists
we feel every inch of our bodies against the air?

She pushes up the hill. From throat, to tongue, to lips,
her lungs beat. Two blue wings under the muscle.

I linger beside the lake. A reservoir circled in asphalt,
in dip and rise. Egret here and there. Stilt dance.
Two months pregnant. My grandfather dying a mile away.

I just need a minute before I go back. I am walking
his dogs while hospice cares for him. I am watching
others lose themselves to the body.

VALENTINE: ON OBSERVING DA VINCI'S SKETCHES OF THE UTERUS

for Paula Gunn Allen

da Vinci's heart is a womb
so full, the child Ohs herself
until her heart presses a mouth
that has yet to breathe: a dust devil rising,
her mother's hair still wet from birthing,
the wind or her own skin.
He etched the delicate heel, arch and crease
of an infant's feet, devoted to the detail.
Each toe a warrior, ready to carry her,
unafraid of the snow falling
in drifts against the house.
I could rock the whole thing in one hand.
My palm covers the vessels beating at the base.
My fingers edge over the opening
to stroke her forehead.
This is life. He took such care to shade it
in a thousand pencil strokes
and I do not dare to touch it after all.
I see now my heart
is the damp outline of a woman,
her vagina as open as it will ever be.

MY LOVER RUNS HIS FINGERS OVER ME

The gash? In surgery, I swear.
Well, actually, it happened twice.
They broke both arms when I was two.
The doctors snapped each limb, then sliced.

My muscles make a funny sound.
A squeak? A tear? The knife is cold.
My arms once looped, a permanent
curve into belly. Now, be bold.

Open my wrist, already. Cut
where the scar still laps into air
and bone. Please, breach the scalpel mark
and tangle of delicate hair.

Don't be afraid. Enter me. Here.

STRINGFELLOW ACID PITS, EMERGENCY DRILLS, AND SMOG ALERTS

Breathless, I see the San Andreas Fault,
as the car curves into the high arc
of the freeway overpass. Gravity presses
the earth, a fissure far below. Yes, we fear
earthquakes the most.

An unpredictable god graces this land,
wants it back, shakes us loose
from time to time.

I am on yet another highway, a long hot trip
between a relative and home. My mother driving
fast when she can, making up time,
in smooth stretches, in bursts.

I think walruses sleep on either side of the road.
Somnolent foothills, dark brown, and rolling.
Then a sudden yellow warning,
toxic waste. This is why god is angry
and wants us out.

Pyrite Canyon crawls up the mountain
above the basin of Glen Avon.
And in this desert, *they dug a hole*
and dumped it in. 34 million gallons.

McDonnell-Douglas, Montrose Chemical,
General Electric, Hughes Aircraft,
Sunkist Growers, Philco-Ford,
Northrop, and Rockwell-International—
the employers of our towns.

A complex mixture: the acids, the chlorides,
polychlorinated biphenyls, pesticides, volatile
organic compounds and heavy metals.

Nose bleeds, emotional distress, insomnia,
cancer and genetic defects leach out.
Groundwater.

In a rainstorm, the pits flood. The dams cannot hold
back the waste. To prevent a disaster,
1 million gallons are released
into flood control channels.

Children wade in, play
in the brown water.

Luckily, my school is one-storied,
with a flat roof. We never expect
snow in the desert. We can practice
ascending ladders in preparation
for the next spill.

Even more common are the smog alerts.

We just rest in the shade of a tree,
or stay indoors and don't worry
that we have worn a skirt in springtime
and the boys can see our underpants
as we climb to safety.

A state of emergency.

ARDITH'S FEAST

I startle when only four fingers emerge
from the weight of the flour. Grandmother.

The bomb has eaten us
down to the heartbeat.

Kneading fry bread, her right hand disappears
into the dough slapped flat as the Salt Lake Valley.

I tug on your skirt
and try to pull
your tongue out
of silence.

She always keeps her other hand carefully covered.
"The sight of two shriveled fingers would frighten you," she whispers.

Tell me the story
of how you have sex
with one hand.

But my thumbs are meager, too.
Each hand holds only a caterpillar of bone.

Tell me how
your sister nursed babies
without arms.

"You want the whole story in the time it takes me to make bread."
She rolls out the dough. The muscles at her wrist pulse.

Tell me you are a woman
just the same. Tell me
you can hold your man

She moved back into the red rocks, the Mormon trail and the snow,
and left the stares of California. Winter keeps out strangers.

with your hips,
the round adobe curve.

She climbed back into the wet shelter where everyone knows
her story. Her brothers and sisters drop with cancer.

My hands hold the bomb
your mother swallowed,
one hot atom at a time.

She transforms atomic dust into children and grandchildren, into me. My hands are our hands, twisted with our genetic truth. Why are parts of us missing?

Tell me
how you made it here,
when the star spun you out
of its nuclear heart.

"Eat the bread while it still shivers with the heat, love."

THE DARK QUESTION

When you dream
the dream of babies,
does each limb slumber
in its place? Every breath
is holy?

Five fingers and five toes. Even the dream catcher
has five strings crossing each other in the light.
The sparrow's beak just so, the raindrop
perfect, and the open mouth of the flea.

The dark question, birth,
what right have I
to bear children
who surely could not be
in the image of God?

Christ opens his mouth all over me. Red
dirt, brown at the back, his mouth
has been filling up. I have no love for him.
The blessed child. The Lord's reflected light.

Dare I be
this blasphemous?
The mark of the devil
marring more
than my hands?

My father and his mother before him. We beget
small thumbs, a lack of arms, and missing fingers. Horror
in the faces of others. Yet, we persist like dandelions
blooming in the sun, our seeds blowing everywhere.

Our perfection varies.

WE SHOOT LAME HORSES

We shoot lame horses.

We shoot the downy muzzle.
We shoot the five point stars,
fire between their eyes.
We shoot the swaying back
that carries us home.

We shoot the boney knee.
We shoot the heart,
still hot with blood.

ADORATION

Unconditional love. Jesus.
Turn the other cheek.

I want your adoration.

The right hand is the hand of agency.
The left touches what we deem unclean.
I am your equal. Your sister.
If you beat me, beat me as such.

You may not backhand me.

I am afraid of the devil, dark as the belly
of a fish opened. Unconditional hate.

Personal. I don't believe in him.
This lack of faith in evil is a sin,
I know, and makes me more afraid,
as I don't believe in sin, as such, either.

The snake eats its tail.

Evil, yes, I have seen it.
It is no temptation.
It does not hunt me.

Christ is but one aspect of love,
of god, though most beautiful.

So the devil must be
but one aspect of hate.

METAPHOR

Today, my scars ache. A reopening. Each needle-sized pinch,
pink prayers on the wrist, all along the jagged break
of arms, and other tears in the surface.

These are not suicide marks. I have never
wanted death. You know, an artist leaves a single flaw,
sometimes more, in the tapestry.

MEDICAL ART

Tumors are roses gone wild
in the heat of the belly.
Their blossoms convulsing pale
shades of raspberry jelly.
Blisters lake together, crop
circles of the inner thigh,
in a solid water dance
tender as a lullaby.
Scars drown the skin by the hip
bone's pit and trace a worm's twine
spinning into hard candy,
ovals above the hairline.
I hold my legs mute under
the doctor's bookish caress,
trying to become still life
in my tissue paper dress.

REOPENING

for my mother-in-law

Under the arm, the skin goes black like the teeth of a comb,
and where her baby suckled, unforgivable
purple merges with yet another shade of blue.
Last year, I knew no one who had lost her breast,
lost the one tangible weight. Now, Sara is the fourth.
Her zippered flesh full of too much color,
yellow here and there, an amazing azure.
I am seeing her for the first time without her shirt.
I am helping to clean the wound. Where is the whiskey
at a time like this? The q-tips are piling up.
Remember when our chests were even with our hips?
The flat xylophone of bone and skin echoing
with playful sweat. Every note in place. Cupped hands,
the only roundness, listening for our bras to fill.
The x-ray hears a different song, a lump
under the areola, a pucker of cells winding their way
back to the dark grace of her lung. The breast,
meaningless against breath, had to go. But where
do all the breasts go? Somewhere there's a pile
of a hundred human breasts, hollow holding hollow.
We talk about the technicalities: lymph nodes,
bruising, the life span of stitches, and grief.
She is flat, stretched taut, waiting again,
remembering how the radiology room went dark,
nipple dark and even the nipple has been removed.

ELSA

You refuse to even try to do a pull up.
You have one good arm.
Every finger strong to the knuckle.
I hang by my chin, gulping.
The metal tang of the bar drifts up my nose.

We are not related although people assume we are
sisters or at least cousins. We are not even friends.
I have candy-corn hair. Your hair is thickly braided
and as brown as the roots of a walnut tree.
You are much prettier than me.

But my shrunken thumbs and oddly curved wrists
parallel your dwarfish right hand. My father warns me
about hanging around others who are different.
We will stand out: two dented cans
among rows of perfection.

LUNCH

I can't open the peanut butter. The lid
marks my palm with a new lifeline,
pink and angry. I will not cry.

The jelly. I want to shatter the jar,
make a grape and glass sandwich.
I try strawberry.

No. My hands are weak. Lord,
have mercy. Let marmalade be the one.
Nothing else to eat in the house.

Why was I born without
the necessary muscle in my thumbs
to make the lids go round?

In dreams, I open everything—
pearl necklaces, cold cream, boxes
of chocolates—with a flick of the wrist.

Tell me thumb-based secrets.
The piano. The snap. The jar.
I am hungry.

THROUGH THE FINGERS

I wish I could lick the rummage of sweat
from my back. My tongue on parts of me
I've never seen. Spine and the two-handed
spread of tailbone guide my skin and now
my mouth. Perfect. Undeformed. Taste.

Open-mouthed and swallowing,
every flawless thing
kept from me.

My lips swell with hunger, throat thick with desire.
I am afraid. Hands streaking to my mouth. Beggars.
They refuse to be ignored. Disorderly, my thumbs pant
in expectation of my tongue. They demand the adoration
reserved for other body parts. I begin at the shoulder.

Then, down the long arm,
slow as spring
up the mountain.

I kiss five hundred hairs and more freckles.
The first scar is tangy where salt gathers.
The wrist has no bone. I suckle the marrow
from the next scar, the zest of needle
still there, a sickle, and a railroad track.

This is the vein to the heart,
threaded
through my hand.

Each finger wet, digested, rubbed against teeth,
known. They are unable. Born reckless in the weight
of their palm, spreading wide to reach over the limits
of my thumbs. Night untangles in the spool-sized gaps
between them, a whorl of stars through my fingers.

Nestled on the tongue,
each thumb
a devotion.

I have never seen them before. Crooked, light
as grasshoppers, and small. No knuckle
to burden them. Fat as a toe. A revelation
of the flesh. I buried them in pockets.
I hid them in the edges of photographs.

LA CHINGADA, EVE, MARY, LA LLORONA, AND DEER WOMAN WALK INTO A BAR . . .

Yucca stand tall, ghosts
are in the graveyard, moonlit
in the desert. Lanterned with white
flowers for eating. Machetes needed
at harvest time.

I think I see Isabel
walking down a path,
kicking dust and small rocks

as we used to do after school
in the dry spring, young,
still just a whisper of girls.

Her shirt billows, loose and thin,
like Flor de Izote petals, but ruined
with dirt and heat.

She is a shadow in my lashes.
Unavoidable tumbleweed.
A drop of sweat I cannot see,
but feel. Perhaps, instead, a tear.

And then she halos, light consumes her.
I blink from too much glare. She is
a refraction of the sun.

An object study. She is not
this poet's rib. She is
a study of sacred texts—
illuminated pages.

All edible flower, monster, and saint.

~

There is sweat in salvation.

It has a certain smell.
Sharp and salted.
Hot car and vinyl seats.
Airless.

Izzy is Salvadoran, pugnacious
jaw and blowzy body, traveled
to America via the road, Quetzalcoatl's
rainbowed trail, Pan American
highway, in the trunk of a blue car.

She told me this, the first day we met.
And also of decapitation, sodomy,
the stink of burning
flesh and cigarettes.

~

I ask her not to stand so close,
to link arms or hands. It's hot
and hard to walk joined
like that.

There will be a comparison.
A compression. Fruit
from the flower.

Who would want such intimacy?

The boys thought she was a slut
because her hips rolled and her breasts
were large, unbound. Her pelvis
slightly crushed at the joint.

She was a little slow of thought from the beatings,
starvation and dissociation. Slow of speech,

a new language on her tongue. She lived
in a group home between the Baptist Church
and the Safeway.

She looked a bit like Mary to me—
the one on the votives you can buy
at any liquor store, but fatter.

She never pretended
she wasn't ransacked,
her father hung, her brother castrated—
that some miracle had saved her,
that she missed El Salvador.

I tried to make sense of her.
La Llorona lived in the gutter,
reaching for Izzy and me.

I don't hate the communion.
I have not been severed
and made whole again. Such things
inspire hate. I am still.

My mother is not well—
screams in the night,
knows agony—
but does not look it.

Izzy is slightly mad.
Her eyes too bright
then suddenly dull.
Everyone knows.

Deer Woman, eyes open, arrow
though the lung,
breathing in, breathing out,

Isabel, a helix forming between us.
Chimera blooming empathy.
Yucca, lay down your spines.

PALPITATIONS

In the space between horror and ecstasy
stretches a common rhythm of blood.

The vessels that guide us
know no difference of emotion:
the sudden knife, a run, and the lover
pushing one more finger inside
all pump the heart wild against the breast.

The heart is a fist and yet it trembles
like a hatchling, flushes hot
and shivers the skin.

How vulnerable, how thin the distance.

When I am aware of the pulse at my wrist, the panic
of blood and muscle of my womb, I don't care what it engorges.

Here is the metaphor for the labia unfurling
and the reason women cut their wrists.
We can't stand the sensation.

GREEN FLIES

We like our beauty singular—
the virgin, the rose, the sun
perfect in their isolation.

The iridescence of green flies captured
in the minute drone of their wings
and their eyes twitching
from a thousand ports
can hardly be called beautiful
when we know their tongues
cast out vomit
when they touch down.

They sting and bite and live three days.
They land on the lip, on shit, on horses,
and then return to jeer the curving ear.

Yet en masse, one inch above the blue ripple
of a lake, gathered in a hover to tease the trout,
they glitter prettier really than pearls or even diamonds
because of their restless breath and buzz.

Those wings fan out and catch the sun.
Their lives translucent swell and shimmer.
Virginity is pointless. The rose an excess
of pollen and passion.

SCARABS

A whole caste
for the cleaning of shit.
Public toilets swept
with the hands.

What are they thinking
as their backs bend?
What are they thinking
as their fingers clutch?

The untouchable.
Dream.
The untouchable.

Beetles have a whole life
of legs on the underside.
We do not see those legs
kick free.

I am a castaway, cleaning
twelve houses a day,
vomit on my hands
from someone else's children.

The untouchable.
Dream.
The untouchable.

VIRGINS

I have never envied a man
standing before the gun of war.

I have always thought it dreadful
that men, with their faces fresh
before that first shave, carry the burden
of their countries on their backs.

Like camels, like elephants, like mules, like dogs.

What is infinite in them bleeding
into the mud, catching
on the trees, burning in the salt
of someone else's ocean.

As if they were *less than*
in some mathematical equation.

Is this not our virgin sacrifice?

For how many of these boys made men
by death and desperate action have slid inside
another's body, shuddered, split open,
and gave the life of themselves?

WHITE-KNUCKLED BEAUTY

Until I saw my first naked man,
I never knew the meaning of vulnerable.

Men smell like tar, sweat, grease and oil at the cuticle.
Their eyes are windblown, skin pocked white and salty.

The beauty in them is sheltered
in the broad madness of their bones

wide as wrenches under the callus
and blister of their work.

I know there are other kinds of men—soft
and dimly lit in cubicles—

but these men did not father me,
don't rub against me in bars

with palms up, the rope and pulley
of muscle extended

to ask me for a dance.
Pure white-knuckled beauty.

The flat spread of ribs, the basketball hard paunch—
a frame women hang their dreams on.

LINGUISTICS

A harlot is a rascal, knave, a fornicator.
At least up until the 1400s,
when a harlot becomes female
and prostrate.

In all language,
we have many words
for what we find delicious,
and this bit of flesh
for sale
is quite the morsel.

Of all the names with which we paint
her red, I prefer just two:
Academia and Swallow-cock.

The first indicts a scholar's knowledge,
a professional expertise at an art.
The second is a crude pun
that transforms her
into some kind of bird,
probably English.

THE VAST

Men are not what I want them to be.
They cannot protect me.

They look at me and open
like a throat

of an anemone
showing the sea its hunger.

We all look like that—
vast and dark

as the ocean
which surrounds us.

I feel vast—
how am I to crawl

between their spines
and hide?

OYSTERS

Rape is accessible,
the statistics high enough
among the disabled
to make us pause
while reading the newspaper.
It is so easy
to push a woman
from a wheelchair
to the ground;
it is so easy to flip
a man over.
We feel the wet breath
on our necks.
Helen Keller lived
in sensation.
What is the sensation
of love? We know
the heel of the hand
either fine or coarse roaming
where it shouldn't,
opening us up
when we don't want to be opened.

JANGLE ME

Under the rose bushes
Sit down low in the dirt
Watch the pill bug flirt
With the teeth marks
On a fly-away paper cup
Don't drown in the 7UP
Bubble sheen lipstick smear
Jangle me clear
Work time five and dime
Not in love with the indent
Of hunger or stress
Careless
Pill bug
Sweet slug
Save this spot for me
Jangle me

MAKING LOVE: A THANK YOU OF THE BODY

Every story is an act of love.
—Dorothy Allison

My tongue knows your breast swallowing my mouth,
your sandpaper nipples, the taste of licorice
along the thigh, the curve of your undelicate ass, your hips
a square yawn in my hands, your dishwater blonde, the salt
of saddleleather at your eyebrows, the shattered vines
where your son pushed through, your dull tumbleweed of pubic hair,
and your bedsheets and minty floss more seductive than a crush
of hibiscus.

Skin, the raw pink of a starfish belly, like a peach
with the fuzz rubbed off, my hand catches your sweat.
You are too wet to touch and come up clean. Your heat suckles me.

Sleep. Sleep. Let your bold tongue lull. You have been brave enough.

CHANT

Deep voices carve song
heavy as the demon
of adultery in the first cycle
of a marriage.

The beat of throat-hum
under throat-hum
waves pale the sopranos
of vespered nuns.

This music is strong enough
to heave the darkness
from the muscles of our shoulders.

Each note,
bone before body.
Hallowed. Full.

This sound can carry us
across the bridge
to unreachable heaven.

A HUMAN SOUND

Why classical music in headphones over the womb?

Why the harp,
the violin,
and maybe the classical guitar,
with its expectant belly?

Not the beat box, washboard, syncopated spoons
and especially not the human voice.

Why must the human voice,
trilling,
bass basic,
joy,
sorrow,
and remembrance
be removed
to build intelligence,
to make space
for thought?

Or we require silence—
no noise of the world.

Cricket and crying baby,
jackhammer and lullaby,
flute, flood, fools laughing.

And yet,
when does our most needed thinking come,
but inside the drum humans, indeliberate, make—

the whine of metal, rubber, and engine plunge
toward us, guns fire, women scream out
their grief, the senator stands up, lights ticking

green, yellow, red, children too loud at the table,
our classrooms, all chalk dust and students, filling up

filling up with the noise
of each world
inside them.

Noise vivid
as lightning,
as bow
to string
as a thought.

VANITY AND BREATHING

If you think vanity is hard on the soul, you should try asthma. Hard to spell and hard to breathe. Mirroring the inside of your body to the outside. Hey everybody! Take a peek. This is my lung. This is my other lung. Over here is the fine rooting twist of my bronchial passage. Next, we have inhaler, steroid, and asphyxiation. Words unpretty, limping around the tongue, getting lost in the peculiarities of taste buds. Not said but read. Blue and red fibers of oxygen, please come in, please come in, my modern ether. No need to be sexy.

DEER WOMAN

We think of her as part of the fawn,
the missing part, as she is often dead,
but really she is just a camouflage,
part of the shelter of the babe
in some sunlit meadow.

Or worse, we harem her.
The bucks so glorious
in rut. She, a quiet, eyes
wet, waiting.

But I am telling you,
the doe is her own
thing. She does her own
thing. She will kick
you down. She tramples,
and somewhere inside,
you know it.

> I am just like a deer
> craving salt.
>
> I tread the shoreline,
> unsure and divine.
>
> A reflection in the lake
> of shadow, sun and mistake.
>
> I am just like a deer
> eating fear.

Deer Woman is a trickster,
a North American mixture,
a fawn-skinned fixture,
a doe-eyed picture.

White tail, brown belly,
leaping the trail.

Her black braids setting sail.
Hoof prints tempt the male.

Ready for her next vault,
sweating salt.

HURRICANE SEASON

The ocean raises its bloom each fall.
The water petals and unfolds into the sky.
Seals dive deep and even the reef trembles.

Gardens of salt and sand flower in the wind.
Each cloud is a row of returning. Each raindrop
is seeded with the original flood.

They say the sea is jealous.
Is not everything its own blossom?

SLEEP

1.
I am an animal,
most days.

Sweat and breath.
Food and sleep.
Warmth and water.
Shit and sex,
but love.

Labor with me,
so we have shelter.
Share a meal
of what we have gathered.

Rest next to me,
body safe.

2.
Like a hummingbird's wings,
so flutter-fast, the moment
our eyes drift shut.

We can't see it or hear it,
nor get close enough
to feel it.

We relax into the uncontrollable
blink—everything suddenly matters less—
and are asleep.

3.
Rippled scallops,
bones of sea.

So at rest, movement
seems impossible.

But flesh and muscle
pull the ocean.

4.
No one likes to wake
a sleeping baby.

The eyelids flutter,
the breath tides even.

We know they sleep only
because the body insists.

And the body is right.

HIEROLOGY

The box turtle is a subtle thing
for all she carries, the world
and its eternities on her back.
Holy mother.

If the land is barren, she holds her young
inside until the season is survivable
for hatchlings and their joyous scramble
of beak, shell, claw and neck.

Plain and brown, the mother,
as any leaf in a pile
and yet, the Gabrielinos warn us,
an earthquake when she argues.

If we glance away, she is lost
to us. She does not have speed,
but she is steady and goes
where she will.

Curious raccoon,
you cannot have her,
no matter how many times
you turn her over in your paws.

A very hungry dog might
be able to gnaw through
carapace or plastron to flesh;
however, it is rarely done.

We will, in lean times, harvest her for soup,
but more often we are voyeurs
to her eating and slight pink tongue—
apostles at her table.

She is here now and will be
here after us. Her children
in the palms of our children.
Trust in the shell that opens.

DECIDUOUS

The maple pities its leaves—
the birdshit and wind, the caterpillar and nesting
ever-singing birds. It disdains the fall—
the new dying—even as it envies
the colors blinding the sun for the reddest red
and the yellow that will stay curled in a child's hand,
a crumpled and still fragment of earth.

But its roots offer comfort
as the leaves tumble, stutter and swirl
to the street and make boats in the gutter—
to become some old man's clutter.

The skin of this poem grows thin
between me and the tree,
or is it me and the leaves.
The leaves and I? The tree and I?

The branches bare shadows
where only loveliness had been.
Winter lasts in monochrome.
We are not always sure
spring will come.

Green joy and the slick beauty
of rain dance out the veins—
hurts a little.

POSSESSION

1.
I own them—jacaranda,
orange, lemon, nectarine
and evergreen.

Ridiculous.

But I will care for them—
sharing water when the rain does not come,
pulling the weeds that might steal from them,
pruning the dead from them,
and in this way, they will be mine—
the way anything is
that we tend
and make tender to us.

2.
I don't like the nectarine at first.
For a long time, I don't know
what kind of tree it is.

I am stupid. The tree will die
if it depends on my care,
my knowledge of what is necessary
for this living thing to thrive.

It is good
that most trees
do not need me.
I hope this one does not.

The tree is not pretty.
It has few leaves.
The emptiness gives
no clues as to what it is.

I do not like not knowing.
I call its former owner.
I have her name all the trees
that shade the yard,
as if I knew none of them,
as if I had not grown up
in dark green groves
of lemon and orange
and picked the purple flowers
of the jacaranda out of the wind
and cut boughs of misplaced evergreen
in our snowless winters.

3.
Crone, you are in my nectarine tree.
Branches, winter-bare and stark,
next to the green show and flower
of the navel orange trees
on either side of you.

Bark, shadow-brown, speckled
with knots and marked by the careless
bite and clutch of animal, bird and bug.

Only a few scrub-ugly leaves adorn you—
too small and yellowed. Each leaf,
pointed like a finger, tries to stretch
and cover a nakedness,
which while not vulnerable,
startles.

The flush of fruit and flower
will be here soon. The tree
will be preposterous
with beauty.

The birds will nest.
We will all eat and scatter
the stones.

But for now, bare, unpretty and bent
it owns itself.

A COSMOLOGY OF HOME

If I were telling the truth, and I should,
I would say to you I am of couches and brown blankets
(all my best blankets have been brown),
hot baths, and uncomfortable chairs for reading,
dining tables of dark scratched wood, and family.

Of sun-dappled light on finger-smudged walls
and the shadowed breeze of ceiling fans, unrepentant
carpet and 1970s parquet, the skid of cat paws down an unswept hall,
the incessant TV, a tumble of music, radio news, my beloved iPhone,
computers and video games, all speaking, beeping and chiming.

And of the bright plastics of toys made cheaply,
plush animal kingdoms, knight, star war, lego, pirate,
block and box, spilled popcorn, and misplaced eyeglasses.

Of the laundry basket, clothing dirty and clean, dishwasher
door ajar, one shoe in the entryway, library books piled
on the living room floor, each sealed in a plastic film
that crinkles for their protection, found buttons, toil,
morning breath, and quick kisses.

I know anyone can make such a list, but this is mine. The truth.
My beautiful crumbs and noise.

Yes, the backyard is lovely. See the winter clover
and the neighbor's lantern tree. The reservoir, ibis in flight
for Christ's sake, more so.

The tamed wild against the sprawling chaparral—my echo.
A coyote running a rabbit to ground, just yesterday, in dusk's light.
The sky, a bonnet. Who could wish for more blue, more shelter?
Clouds to nourish and quench.

And I adore even the ants and the gophers. Foxtails in socks.
Blooming Datura.

The rattlesnake is my sister, never doubt it, I wept
when an incautious car spread her flat and dead
against the summer-sticky road just in front of our home
and teenage boys and some grown men too pulled over
to see her rattles, her spine, and her blood.

But I left her there for the night and the crows
and showed my son my sorrow and her coils.

I know this litany is more interesting—the heart beats faster.
My language shows my love of dirt and death, and of the sun
making me sweat and spinning the world. But here, look again;
there is as much joy inside as out, as much grief. I stand
with the wind—in it and out of it, again and again.

Home is made by human hands. Brick and mortar.
Housed fire. Cotton spun. Weather warded.
Pen and ink. The peace of my husband's heat
in our bed. Our child running in and out of doors.

We are full-bellied, dry, and warm.
Luxury, even, in the meat and chocolate.
There are no unnecessary dangers.

Joy comes sweet as oranges—
I picked them just outside
and brought them in.

SHOALING

for Chris

We can't be without
the ocean. We live
in the Pacific
Rim. The sun is west.
The sea is of dusk,
crown, and corona—
the luminance
simple, anointing.

The surge comes in foam
first, and then the ebb
into the eddy,
whitewater current,
the transverse breaking,
gravity pulling
back into the crest,
through sundark barrel,
trough, wave again, calm
water, confluence
barely out of sight.

If we will just lay,
shoaling, toes to sky,
heels digging the sand,
in the salt-wet sally
of the vast and us,
we will be weightless,
buoyant with the slack.

It will burn a bit,
amplify the sore
we have forgotten,
a resurrection.

Submission is not
necessary nor
surrender, but don't
fidget. Heal, hold on
to the surf and hands
extended to us.

The tide combs through us—
cold, shivered, cleansed.
Waves will rise again,
stigmata assured
but this sweet, fresh joy
of startle and wash
can't be retaken.

WATER BODY

In the thickness of water, my tongue swells.

Shells and salt clump my hair like seaweed
against the suddenly brown earth. Penguins

have a gland for the conversion of the sea
into a body of libation. I know my body

is mostly water. Each cell, a liquid life,
spreading into the heat of another. Jellyfish

float with open mouths. They are the scientist's
Medusa—boneless and hungry. The spray stings

my peeling feet, the veins flaring to the surface
in my thighs, and the deepening purple of scratches

behind my knee. Under my hands, two turtles dig
away from shore, merging the darkness

of their bellies with the sand. Again, I dive
into the stretched skin of a wave.

UGLY THINGS

I am one of those—a person who
reads the end of a book first.

Are you?

Did you turn to this page before any other?
Or are you arriving here last instead of again?

When I declare this habitual motion
of mine to any bookish crowd or personage,
sprawled on the red sofa of a coffeehouse,
down the quiet aisle of a library, over small sandwiches
at book club, gasps follow, some nods and such derision,
a lack of understanding, well-cultivated between
those like us and those like them—
whoever we all are
in this equation.

Of course, I don't consume
the last page of picture books
before the first. Monsters in boats,
the lost sad bunny—I trust them.

Picture books are for children,
mostly. We know their limits.
They will be comforted,
at least, in the low lovely
tones of the end. It is certain.

Poems, too, are read in order
of development,
but that is not because of trust.

Poems tend to be short.
I can endure what happens.

I can risk it. No matter what,
it won't last long, even Dickey's
"Falling." I can handle a singularity:
poem, picture, story.

But suspense is no longer for me.
I don't need it in my imagination
like I don't need roller coasters
anymore. Created terror. Practice.
If real horror hits, I receive it.
I am good at it.

When a book opens
with a baby dying—
I am looking at you,
Louise Erdrich—
not in the normal ways,
if there is such a thing,
well, I don't expect
the baby to come back,
unless it's that kind of novel,
but I do need to know
if anybody else lived
through it and if they didn't,
I need to know that too.

You might think I'm childish.
I am not.

My son, a child of four, announces
he only likes ugly things. Sharp teeth,
the color black, dirt, scabs, exhaust
from trucks—he collects them.

I tell him all of these things
can be quite pretty as well.

They shine, stars inhabit them,
brown smells good, the crust

of blood means healing, vapor
dances in cold air.

He growls. He does not like it
when two things are true at once.

We are in the car. I am driving,
admiring the sunset. I cannot see
his eyes, but I know they are blue
and gleeful as he continues his quest
for even uglier things: dog drool,
scribbles, a sinkhole eating an RV.
He is enjoying himself and I him.

At dinner, I have him list all his ugly
things for his father—lint, snake hole,
scat, spike, Bunyip, bone—who also laughs.

And in our bed, with our son fast asleep
between us, his breath, our breath,
I stay awake long enough to tell
my love this feeling of knowing
this good thing will happen.

One day, our son will know
horror, like the tongue knows
the teeth. We all do.

But we also know
there will be comfort.
We are ready.
We have practiced.
He is not alone.

Acknowledgments

I want to thank City Works Press for creating a collective that allows one writer to assist another. I am also grateful for every poet who has been kind enough to take me as a student and those who apprenticed me unknowingly with their words laid out in books. I am honored by the commitment, tenderness, and honesty each of my companion poets in this book has given this project, these poems, and me. I am indebted and glad to be so. I want to state my deep appreciation to my beloved colleagues as well. Thank you for taking a bit of my usual labor into you so that I could do this other important thing for a while. And for the wise women of my Wednesday nights, I am forever thankful and so pleased to be able to acknowledge you here. My husband and my son gave me time, a little quiet, and patience. I could call it support but it is more than that. Thank you to the many hands that helped me shape and make this book.

Here is the litany of names: Edna, Heather, Liane, Evelyn, Lethien, Nancy, Jamie, Chris, Michelle, Rae'ah, Cindi, Pam, Ella, Kenny, Paul, Cara, Renee, Kelly, Henry, Glover, Micah, Kia, Ray, Adrienne, Sandra, Maxine, Robin, Carla, Sam, Sheri, James, Gay, Rowena, Lynda, Rita, Sabrina, Sara, Louise, Jim, Marilyn, Paula, Danielle, Joy, Andy, Emily, Shelly, Dorothy, Franklin.

Poetry is a strange passion, I am told. It makes little money. Readers have to work too hard. And yet you have read this book and made something of it, I hope. Thank you, dear reader, most of all.

Notes

"Lyric in the Light" epigraph comes from the title of Kenny Fries' memoir *Body, Remember* and originally from the opening line of C.P. Cavafy's poem "Remember, Body. . . ."

"Matilija Poppy" the lines detailing the plant are lifted and fractured from Summitpost.org's "Wild Flower Guide—Santa Monica Mountains."

"Wail" epigraph comes from the second line in Joy Harjo's "Fear Poem" originally published in *She Had Some Horses*. She often performs this poem with her band in full voice behind her.

"Apocalypse" epigraph comes from Paul Verlaine's "The Art of Poetry" as translated by C. F. MacIntyre.

"Liminal" is forthcoming, in a slightly different form, in *The Far East Magazine*, So Say We All, 2012.

"Valentine: On Observing da Vinci's Sketches of the Uterus" was published in *Ekphrasis,* Frith Press in Spring 2003.

"Stringfellow Acid Pits, Emergency Drills, and Smog Alerts" most lines detailing the Stringfellow Quarry Waste Pits and the rainstorm of 1978 are lifted and fractured from the BookRags.com's "Stringfellow Acid Pits."

"Ardith's Feast" was published in *The Beloit Poetry Journal* in Winter 2000.

"Green Flies" was published, in a slightly different form, in The *Externalist: A Journal of Perspectives,* August 2007.

"Linguistics" the opening lines are fractured from Tom Dalzell's *The Slang of Sin*, specifically from entry for harlot.

"Making Love: A Thank You of the Body" epigraph comes, roughly, from *Two or Three Things I Know for Sure* by Dorothy Allison.

Pacific Standard Time

Sabrina Youmans

For anyone who tries to make sense of loss.

"To attach oneself someplace to nature, to that which is strong, striving and bright with unreserved readiness, and then to move forward in one's efforts. . . . Each time we thus reach out with joy, each time we cast our view toward distances that have not yet been touched, we transform not only the present moment and the one following but also the past within us, weave it into a pattern of our existence, and dissolve the foreign body of pain whose exact composition we ultimately do not know."

—Rainer Maria Rilke

Contents

We Are Made of Light

"The universe is made of stories, not of atoms."
—*Muriel Rukeyser*

LACUNA

Noun: gap or missing parts

a. Anatomy: one of numerous minute cavities in the substance of bone

b. Botany: an air space in the cellular tissue of plants

In black and white
my parents fight on the patio.
My dad in a bleached tank top,
my mom in dark cigarette pants.

They search
for something in each other
to only find it missing.

Even bone has open spaces.

My parents divorced in the '70s.
Leaving behind a single image
of them outside yelling.

Afterwards, I found my father
crying in the garage,
curled like a C
in sepia tones
as amber-muted sun
filtered through the only window.

And then he was gone.

His new downtown El Cabrillo
apartment screamed bachelor
with its black leather furniture, digital clocks
and silver balls suspended on strings.
Only Butterfingers and pickles kept
company in the refrigerator.

When truth is unimaginable we concentrate on things.

The event that changed everything
remains untold. After a recent family dinner,
I asked how we kids learned of their separation.
My mom silent, my oldest sister
recalled the details of how she told us.

Ear pointed to the central line, waiting
for someone to explain the unimaginable.
We can never hear loss.

Listen to what is unsaid.
Like the gritty texture
of a pear's vulnerable white flesh.
Protected, wrapped in thin chartreuse
skin, until ripe.

Just a few summers ago
at lunch mom told us
about the redhead. She found
lipstick, and my father
confessed he had to know
what it would be like. How
it would be different.

The truth has no witness.

The pear's flesh slips away,
soft with bruises and brown flecks,
of sweet, too-sweet spots,
that collapse under touch.

Leaves are also filled with tiny holes.

When the body peels away
from the other it knows,
it remembers the damage.

In the cavities between us, we either connect or become lost.

My mom's garden, above the canyon,
struggles to grow strawberries and tomatoes.
There is plenty of sun but the soil is acidic.

Spaces also make room for want.

The blocks of wood
my dad cut and sanded
for us lay scattered on the
gray cement driveway.

We can never fill our loss.

I see her image, dark lipstick
holding quiet, so as not to
breach the unspoken,
the unrevealed,
the impenetrable.

We all tell the stories we want.
My father's entire face animates
talking over coffee—
eyes, mouth, brows
all shifting angles.

Fantastic narrative
spools that loop and fill
or skip and drop
to make more gaps.

We only speak the unspeakable when there are no other options.

The missing is all inside me
the untold, the uncertain
the faraway looks.
I hold their story in my gaps.

The hollows make it stronger.

I finally recognize me,
in a body, my mom's body,
our bottoms round and full
our chests delicate and narrow
a pear inside each of us.

I was fruit and now I am flower.

HEAVY LIFTING

1.

I open my chest to the sun and point my crown to the clouds
bang my butt to the ground, legs like jackhammers, and balance like a bird.

Muscle through it—hoist that barbell upward.
Head down, miss the shoulder shrug, the jump, I'm scared
to drop below the bar—form be damned.

2.

I remember my mom smashing a baking dish against the patio.
It shattered into slivers of white—the scream she never released.

3.

This red-alert anger happened with my lover
at his favorite restaurant, The Reservoir.
He confessed to enjoying being a bachelor too much.

I excused myself for the restroom and in the stall
my neck slung low and deep. I moaned like a thrush in the woods.

4.

In the mirror the dentist held, I could see the theater of my mouth
my squat molar cracked, marked with a black fault of bacteria.
I leaned back and it was drilled to a stub.

My tongue, so strong, tried to fight the invader;
the hygienist restrained it with a fabric noose
to attach the new crown.

The precision of teeth against the sloppiness of mouth.
Fitting together these tight orderly crevices—
my jaw now feels and moves differently—my bones and teeth no longer mine.

5.

I want to cleanse my home with daffodils—
welcome spring with bright yellow anticipation.

I wanted us to work and it changed. So now I welcome change.

6.
Full moon
I want to swallow the oval
roll its white grittiness against my cheek
wrap my body around its curve
swallow it and hold its luminance.

7.
Head up, crown to sky, chest open and full,
shoulders slotted down into my ribs,
fusing my whole body together—
a stance of grace, awareness,
I lift with ease
and balance; position myself for inevitable difficulty
take it in, don't fight or ignore it,
absorb the white heat of effort, risk and pain.

UNION STATION

1.
Your attention please,
I have a plan.

The horizon is here
within me.

The equator swirls
true through my compounds—
heart to ribcage to spine.

The want, the desires
dissipate like a fading arch.

2.
We recognize movement;
at profound moments we imprint—
on a Ferris wheel, a stranger's green-checkered shirt
next to clouds that build like cabins in the sky.

We see joy and make a path
to feel the moment again and again
to continually shape ourselves in the world.

Our chemical selves,
our chemical nature.

3.
I am not always as capable as time.

As sure as the horizon seems,
I search for a comfortable place in this courtyard.

Where water gathers near the train's moan,
the urge passes.
A second goes by against
the yellow burn of an endless day.

Comfort in the blue and green
similar sisters of calm
terracotta tiles locked into a pattern
together in squares and triangles.

4.
Against the city
gray and multilingual with self-interest.

Rest here and collect our thoughts,
rinse them in the fountain.

5.
Trees wrapped in twinkle lights,
a mirage of destination to encourage marriage
among the trains.

Paragons of schedules,
of coming and going,
of counting.

Let me tally who I am:
a broken bird feeder,
an exhausted seeker,
a daughter calling.

6.
No need to look too far for accuracy.
The pattern of blond hair on arms
is most reliable.

Moles, scars, a road map—
lay a thousand bodies together
and a new pattern emerges.

7.
That morning you wrote a message on the bathroom mirror
tracing into the mist, we disappeared just as easily.

8.
Locomotives circle around.
Safe. Enough.

9.
The way the sun hits at a slant,
passes through the glass table top,
shadows the ironwork
for a bird dancing underneath,
doused in sunlight and stripes.

Time washes over me, and I steal
a piece and take it in and shape it
into the curves of this memory to sustain me;
this moment layers into other moments.
To track it makes sense
endorphin bread crumbs, a way to
find ourselves, know ourselves.

10.
This moment,
connecting to other times in the sun,
anticipating travel,
becomes a brilliant
sensation
golden bird wings flap inside.

Feeling white-roses-good
olive trees beckon to places
I want to be.

11.
Not feeling hungry or needy.
Just waiting at Union Station,
opening a problem, a thought,
against an accordion of stained-glass images,
to look at and to consider.

FOUR GRACES: A BLESSING FOR THE WORLD

May we learn from pine,
sycamore and spruce
how to take pleasure in giving
shade, offering to filter air
while holding steady
as wind blows
the community of green
freely so each leaf maintains
concentration and connection
to know when to change
or when to produce fruit and seed.

All the kindness and the virtue
of trees lives in us.
May their elegance
remind us of our own
simplicity
and guide us away from
the desire of empty collections:
coins, cars, and companions.

Instead, follow
the texture of their
dimpled gray bark
to the outstretched branches
emanating from each trunk.
Every arm offers the wisdom
of noticing
ladybugs, sparrows, oranges and heat
each holding the
deep satisfaction
of living.

1. To find the wisdom of trees, cultivate pleasure

What we do for others remains.
So live well—rest long hours under the September
sun to warm and relax each muscle
giving, giving,
ripples of warmth,
opening all senses to notice
the barely pink peony
floating in transparent water.

The rabbit offering her body,
the hare's shape on the moon—
sharing evening mangos
yellow, sweet and unassuming.

2. Provide moments of concentration

Our bodies,
contoured temples
that hold the urge to achieve—
toss each bale of hay
a bit further next time—
also need rest
to soak in
the ease of joy
against the difficult edges
of want
so both brush us
like passing leaves
in a stream.

3. Vapor: The connection between earth and sky

The face of a lake
holds glassy serenity while
sheltering deeper waters

providing clean ways
to see the world
after a choice.

A difficult decision to leave one place for another.
Trading the teal of Mission Bay's inlet
for the freshwater lake in Baton Rouge.

Stand along the shore,
investigate the emptiness,
plumb the depths,
drop the weighted string,
feel its vibration
down spine, tendon,
femur and calf.
Listen to the tone
of the echo
from empty places.
It may sting.
See things as they are.

A woman. A mist rising making a pathway
upwards. The time to return to salt water.

A moment to become familiar with all states of being,
depletion, unsure, resplendent.

4. The lesson of doves: Treat every creature with kindness and justice

The bridges over LA's Venice Canals
stand graceful, strong, ornamental—
purpose suspends us all.
Holding hands.
Wanting to hold hands.
Wanting to understand
the person we want to love.

It does not matter why he prefers two pillows—
there is pleasure in giving him two down squares
to rest his head.

The boundless ocean melts,
limitless, a common
waterway we all ride.

We are fish
that make up the blue
of the ocean.
Dolphin curving out of this surface,
arcs of happiness
light bouncing off
rubbery skin.

What will you give?
Everything.
The wind collects all of it—
lost eyelashes, seed abundance,
the tensile strength of floss,
the burden of pollution,
the levity of pollen—
all passes through
persimmon feathers
of a hummingbird
who whips the gathering forward.
The most potent elements cling to its wings
gaining import.
We pause to appreciate
when the blue sky filters
light
to become lavender—
the sublime
belongs to all of us.

Our world surrounds us,
cares for us, spirits us, adores us.

Beneath the weeping willow
a jade green heron
poised in solitude.

Her neck traces the curve of water,
absorbs its beauty, echoes more beauty
in a state of grace
that extends all blessings,
moments of joy,
folded into daily life.

ABUNDANCE

Pancakes hot, steamy and fluffy each morning.
Fruit that ripens with touch.
Windows that remain clean.
A cat that is dog-like: pants, licks, and appreciates.
A place to store my thoughts in the cupboard.

Sheets that feel like tropical breezes.
A rock that turns to water when needed.
Pumpkin smash bread from the Indians in the Everglades.
An expansive mind that sees beyond my own needs and wants.
A gecko in my bathroom to sing to me in the shower.

Extensions of thoughts
held frozen in the air
with translations
so we can all understand.

Endless popcorn that comes out of birds' beaks as they chirp.
To be me and not to be afraid.
My house and laundry self-clean and my orchids always bloom.
To understand the purpose of unequal.
    Carrots, peas, and beans,
    different only in texture
    share the same spot on the dinner plate.
    The same is true for a knife, a fork, and a spoon,
    different shapes, weights.
    Their purpose may vary with food
    but all are the same—
    to eat, to help eat.

My next car will be electric and clean
because I will not be in a rush,
and I will not eat in it.
I will keep a spot of the sun in my locket.

I am in brown sugar arms tonight.

A way to fly around the world
so it will always be sunny.
My apartment grows into a home—
those plastic blinds are really plantation shutters.
I do things the right way.

Trees reach down and touch my hair
sensing sorrow. They also bend
their branches around me.
Woodsy and loved.

Mass transit in LA from the Westside to Downtown.

Hot tea tastes as good as it smells.
That concrete becomes soft when running on it.
I can climb a tree
do a backbend
and fly a kite
all on the same summer day.

IT JUST GOT SIMPLER

He calls on his way to Broken Top Mountain to describe what he sees:
"A green pasture with three horses, a bald mountain and some cows."
I tell him what I saw that morning walking Tecolote Canyon:
"The daisies are waist high, lavender, yellow, and white!"
They form a sea of blooms against a field of deep mustard and green hills.
I tell him what I see feels like, as Neruda said,
what he does to my heart.
He whispers, "One pony just sauntered over to nuzzle."
Everything just got simpler.

"Taken as a whole" is the phrase that circles my mind over and over.
He takes it all. My breath and my ideas that are too wild to contain.
When I randomly drop silverware in the dishwasher basket, he suggests
putting them upside down so the utensils can sanitarily
be returned to their place in the drawer.
This seems like too much trouble, and is anything really clean?
But I nod. And smile.

I make a mental concession. But do not change.
I like things the way they are.
I make everything seem so balanced and so appealing,
but 700 miles stands between me in LA and you in Bend, Oregon.
You tell me not to come, You're back with your ex.
Shattering the pool of calm surrounding me.

He knows this and traces my mind with his fingers,
along its curves and contours;
he sees the world in perfect and imperfect circles as I do,
soft, overlapping ovals
around us, our thoughts.

He walks around me, circling, and we are not quite ready.

FOUR CORNERS

There are four corners to every state.
Edge, border, boundary and line.
All endure the demarcation, except original people.

Here in Montana
the ground shrinks
under the unfolding weight of the sky.

Profiles of clouds combine,
suspend, and stare back
so it's hard to tell

a nimbus cloud from a mountain top
a dark crag from a bison
or a run-away goat from a small car.

Here shoulders square
walking down one
of many Main streets.

We share fair portions of strawberry
rhubarb pie, quarters of field to mow
as our four heart chambers fill.

Here the weather changes with force.
Equal shares of melting sun, slapping wind,
restless dust, and sudden condensation.

It's all part of making a dust cake:

1. Mix dry ingredients
2. Blend wet items in their own bowl
3. Mix together, and
4. Bake (it's all chemistry)

Along the Bitterroot River
four steps from the shore
my hand meets a bleached stone.

Fingers find comfort around
this hot dry skull
cousin to the many craniums

scattered by the waterway
each tumbled forward from the past
by the indifferent current.

All of these bone-colored rocks line the river bed;
there was once hope to find a route,
a waterway

to cross the Northwest passage
to divide mountains
with ease and offers of prosperity

only to find
there is no easy way
and other people already live here.

In my hand the stone
has four indentations
Lewis, Clark, temple and jaw.

Almost all my fingers wrap around
the globe to connect with
Salish, Blackfoot, Flathead, and Kutenai

while local shirtless bored boys
skip rocks to see
what happens when

solids meet liquid
with velocity
and grace.

Trees look to the sky
for answers to find only
dawn, dusk, noon, and midnight.

GRAVITY

The moon, a slice of my bones,
floating high & round
luminous inside & radiating out.

I see a sliver of me in the universe
a bit of humanity in the skies.

The particles, particulates, we populate space
our eyes the stars, our thoughts careen like asteroids
& we find ourselves in the heavens as we are on earth.

Gritty like sand, my tooth in the moon,
that texture of dejection
covers the surface of my mouth.

Here it is, lost & distant, beautiful.
A piece of me
connected to the galaxy
by a hair, by gravity, by stories.

In heaven as in earth
the sacred is
knowing
the now
& being
comfortable
seeing ourselves
as bits
of the moon's light.

Back on the lawn,
my face to the grass
Whitmanesque,
inhaling the green,
free-floating

cellulous in the air
liberating, undulating,
bringing me home
to the earth
ready to catch me.

Evaporating water releases
minerals that male butterflies
need during mating season.

Cold-blooded, they bask
sun-besotted on hot rocks
heat & steam
warming wings for flight.

Each opening & closing
of their matched pennants
release desire
into conspicuously
marked appendages

similar structures that
gods, angels, demons, and even shuttles
use to take flight.

Chasing butterflies,
our wanting
may be expected
but impossible to obtain.

We may never have everything we need.

THE TRIBE IGNITES

Poised over LA's Venice Canals
an ancient benevolent pine
hosts hundreds of lanterns

reaching its evergreen arms
over saltwater channels
surrounded by eclectic

narrow palaces.
Positioned just over a
bridge in witness, in guidance.

Each branch drenched
in metal boxes, luminaries,
in gold, wrought iron, patina

and tin. Bell shapes
from Paris streetlights,
fluted Moroccan pendants,
hexagonal columns echo

India, celebratory
cylinders call from China,
all hold the shapes of
wise ancient faces.

At night the tribe ignites,
forming a halo
of blessings, hallucinations.

Let us experience
her clean heat
of the unbearable.

Survive that nagging sense
that something is missing
in the resplendent prisms of light

now shining requiems
for the lost and the found.

We drink the light
and rotate inward,
lit from within
as a lantern.

All passageways
gleam,
emit no heat,
just perspective
with direct eye-line
to see
the tumble of beasts
crawling inside us,
see it all for what it is
and survive,
come through stronger than
we think we are.

Each lamp suspended
on this wise evergreen
becomes a chime
that rings
awareness
brings acute lenses to see
the smooth rich lines of rapture
and the stark broken jots of devastation
that makes us and unmakes us.

Each transparent globe,
bearing within a story,
a meaning burning with the
intention of interaction.

Connect to their afterglow
so we no longer need to repeat
the tranced pace of loneliness.

Be brave, let people be people,
take in the scales
the hooded eyes
the missing words
shine the light on
each awful moment
as proof of existence—
place the dreamy and the unbearable
side by side under the same lamp.

Lotus shaped,
each lantern escorts
lost souls,
ripe fruit dropping from the tree,
landing where most needed.

California Incline

"We do not see things as they are. We see things as we are."
—*The Talmud*

WE BUILD

Tonight, you,
an actor/comedian
and me, a poet/teacher,
press our bodies,
our lives together
and a city grows
from our tangled forms
under an ocean comforter
not far from the 405.

Girders and pulleys
hoist us, twist us,
constructed of movement.
With each 2 x 4 we become
skyscrapers aching
to rise and rise again—
our backs undulating bridges
foundation and air.

Your hands, sky roofs, and fans,
ventilate and spin.
I settle you; pull you closer,
conveyer belts and elevators rise,
in tones of grays, sepias, putty and buff.

Folding in, doubling, rebounding,
a gymnasium, warehouse, laundry facility.

New empty spaces
offer the porcelain coolness of tubs,
we lie alongside each other,
subway systems, sewers and light posts—
we become infrastructure—
our elbows buttresses, our noses vents.

We stand street lamp over telephone wire,
our toes sidewalk crack upon asphalt planes.

We grind our bodies and churn out
blueprints of hardscapes—
you concave into my neck
installing an irrigation system.

I pull away, hallways and corridors,
abound. You pursue me with smooth boards,
planks for stairs for our stoop-cum-
wrap-around porch.

I search for crystal handles on
dovetailed drawers,
window jambs perfectly squared,
but you may have to go further back.
Before the clubs and the stages.

We reside here among the crafted,
in the way things work,
tight corners jointed together in purpose.

Or here in the freshly sawed naked wood
of a new door at our threshold
opening to space and more space;
we pause before entering.

We claim this unknown city
for each other
stake a flag
colored in my pinkish cream
of blanched almonds
against your radiant
clay after a rain.
My pale areolas,
peonies against
your new-branch bronze,
merge into a bird's herringbone back feathers.

Where we join
there is trust and anti-trust;
our words form a series of arches
holding torque.

We still make indentations
from the weight
of our bodies, bones and organs.

My fingers circle your chest curls, spinning
them into communities, schools, churches and shops.
From our touching abdomens spring
universities and global industries,
archives for museums, campuses and ballparks.

Exhausted, our breath forms a drape around us,
a canopy of catacombs,
secret spaces, nooks, and safe houses.
We rest and take in
the image of our expanding
tentative fawn of us
unfolding from the sod
legs impossibly bent and frail,
odd angles straighten to stand;
we hesitate, falter,
then balance.

Mesmerized, I eat popcorn from a big blue bowl
and wonder where you are tonight.
Not in our city, but hopefully arriving soon.
Expected at the rising arm of the station,
you'll be late by two hours and I won't care
because that is how the system works in our city hall.

My hips hold the light to show us the way
when things are muddled.
Your hips are responsive pivot points,
transitional zones.
Our chests are the

passageways
to our temples, sanctuaries,
where our minds host rushes of mushroom,
cabbage clusters,
birds so brown and black
that they are mistaken
for polished wood, leather,
even marble fixtures
until we move through them
causing scatter
when our bodies adjust.

There will always be this place of us.
I dream it with each touch.

Now we have the blueprint
of how to build it together.

STONE FRUIT

In the season of stone fruit
everything seems lighter.
The air heats and rises lifting us
closer to the sun, bodies spread
apart, bones seep away from joints
humidity swells open spaces
so there is room for things unimaginable.

That perfect firm deep red sweet
beyond what is possible
a tang in the ripe of the mouth
to linger
notice the sublime
the ease
the sway
the sun drenched and dappled
on empty dusty roads.

The longer slower sleep
with windows open
fan scanning
blowing away discomforts.

When the trees
offer a taste inside their soul
they make more
and more and more
nectar
holding not just water,
but tomorrow;
in this season of tilting back
the breeze takes voices
into the trees.

We are all here
absorb the same sun
melt a little from the wanting.

The seasons carry on
the stone
the essential
seed of being.

We feel looser and lighter
come June
when the sun holds us
opens all
a slowing
a gift
flesh ripens just before rot
trees struggle in their abundance
birds feast
on the ease of flesh
loosely attached to the stone
white plum or clingstone cherries
hold on with their skins
are more juicy than tender.

Summer
finds us
sometimes we await
sometimes it catches us by surprise.
Simple fruits, ripened from a single flower
impossible to possible
sweet flesh folds
around an essential center.

COME AGAIN, WINTER

I remind myself
with each falling leaf
that change
is in our nature.

The fading autumn sun
ushers in the release
of more leaves—
a rain of papery gold.

I skip among
the floating
gilded petals
that drape us
in surrender.

I want to
say the blades
have bravery
but they do as
they are.

They face change
with fluttering
ease and grace.

The wind
offers
a hushed
refrain
that lilts with
each falling
arrow:

  Let go
  dance
  free

drift down
and welcome
loss
in release
in response.

I float among
these tree feathers
noticing how their
sacred remains
gather and thatch
upon once-bare sidewalks.

It is with reassurance I hear:
The green will return—
spring is always here
inside each tree.

Winter, you are welcome.
Take us.
Our saffron
flowers
belong to you
drop in your honor.

Come again, winter,
we shed for you.

Let us make room
for your clean cruelty.

Come again, winter,
we wave you close.

We release each kin,
a triangle ship
drifting
downward
layering into

a comfortable
bed.

Come again, winter,
it is time for you—
we are change
and we are ready.

MAMMOTH

The road points us toward the seam between
mountains; my eyes roll up and along the textures.
Darkness drops around us; only the snow holds a glow.

As we drive home, the motion reminds me of how
skiers lean into the slopes as the mountain leans
into the night—my hips point east and then west

while I glide down the incline, swish, cut, swish
a disorienting moment, blue to white, to purple,
only to discover I can no longer ski.

Instead, I write on a split of wood with gloves,
sitting next to and among frozen crystals
that create a delicate drip-hum of constant melting snow.

I walk, and the crunch of each step
gives into a letting go as I surprisingly
sink ankle deep—the earth wants me close.

There is an audience of bare birch trees,
like attentive spectators, and of course the sun sees all
the beauty and I turn and twirl in it.

The thrumming of dripping ice almost staccato now,
thick and deep as it hits tundra—the earth
absorbs each drop with a ping.

A man walks across the meadow with his black dog—
the animal reluctant and unsure of all except his master's voice.
It reminds me of us.

You are afraid as we lead each other;
what I want waits a day until you are ready,
until the idea of us, like raw dough, is baked in your mind.

Will that be our pattern? The way the snow falls unevenly on us?
How you expertly ski each slope,
carving an emotional time zone between us.

The way a pine branch laden with snow bends down, lower,
until the weight of the flakes falls gently off,
sloughed like a sweater no longer needed?

Do ice grains and air and breath and beauty all carry love?
This is my simple and profound blessing—
to toss snow into the sky and see the sun through it.

Like you, the snow does not absorb, but reflects light.
A kind of deceit. I am still waiting to name you,
elusive, the nickname needs to be fitting—

lean bear, tentative, caring and constant.
We will name each other when we know.
Until then we wait and travel and

dodge and walk and kiss;
the names will arrive just as we did.
Sudden, pleasant, a surprise, fitting.

And then another layer of snow descends to cover it all up again.

BETWEEN STATES

I've spent years
between locations
waiting for forces to propel me
into another state
or take me back.

Hovering uncertainty
not sure if it is hunger or thirst
an orange or water,

longing or boredom.
Is that phone light blinking red for me?

Discontent
air-conditioned induced chill.

Unease
pulling tight across the bottom of my ribs
until the moment confronts us.
I understand you cannot love me
and
I can't wait until you do.

Always there are
places
in between places
airports
to see
things as they are.

I have gathered myself
and my things. I am no
longer in transit.

I am tired of safe and lonely
or exciting and lonely.
Suspended but not connected.

A thoughtful, if delusional place.
I've been here too long.
It has cost me years
and a child.

In a casino parking garage
next to your white dented car
I danced near your open window
in a blend of humiliation and hope
caught between myself and the idea of me.

I have traveled so long
from that weekend in Vegas
to end up back in baggage claim.
Where steel petals roll and fold.
Roll and fold
in a calming rhythmic way.
It's almost too much, too mundane,
sublime even.
It awakens my pride.

In my chest cage where I store my failure,
I realize my sense of love
cannot be both real and imagined.
It doesn't matter how you feel
but what you do.

Sitting in this place, orbiting my life
from a plastic chair—I decide.

I am the force
the attraction
causing terrestrial
bodies to fall toward center.

LUNAR HOUSE

When the glorious orb rises
the ocean pulls our hair
dragging us back to our origins.

Women cycle, slough and start again.
A mini-revolution—
this body renewal
that continues existence.

A celebration really,
so I refuse to be put aside,
considered a mess.
There will be no moon house.
There will be sex.

My lover and I follow the milky lunar shine
in stages, his body rounds mine,
our silken clean mouths attach
and we join in all liquids: water, salt and blood.

This moment of convergence
so different for so many.

Some cultures separate
the bodies for a week
after the bleeding.
A ritual bath reunites.

My Pacific Palisades friend
married an Israeli soldier.
She shared her take on the
practice of Niddah,
not to be misunderstood
as rejection of unclean women,
but as a way to honor the passing of life
and to stoke desire.

I see through her ballerina green eyes,
but I also see through my blue ones.
I do not wish for seven days of separation,
I have had years of being alone.

Still other cultures view men as the
purveyors of women.
My friend from Algeria with welcoming almond eyes
married a man from Morocco who said to her,
"How would you know that you're beautiful unless I told you?"
While I originate from different soil,
hearing this, anger forms in the shape of a gun.

I stare down the barrel of anguish
tired of living in a world where
it is easier to gaze at a woman
than to see a woman.

Beauty and intimacy are easily confused.
The men in my life vary
from tokens of pleasure,
to convenient creations,
and I have yet to transcend
to merging lives while maintaining selfhood.

My bedroom contains the evidence.

Artifacts from lost men—
a gray empty bowl from Thailand,
a circle of dolphins from Los Cabos,
sugary floral pink perfume,
and a silver-knotted necklace
too heavy to bear,
all remnants of male indifference and neglect.

My eyes, drawn to the shapes of choices,
rest on the window ledge lined in colored bottles
tall, ambitious and confident, almost angry,
sure of form, but not true to mine.

The men I pick tend not to be ready.
Safe houses, but not offering a home,

I leave men and hold on to glass.
Neither fulfills.

I will try to see men as they are, not as I want them,
and to choose wisely.
Gloria Steinem believes marriage is the biggest
gamble a woman can make.

I practice looking beyond their handsome gleam
and into their thick masculine walls
that protect and obscure.

I also see me as I am.
More interested in shaping a world
than sharing a life.

I take the challenge
to listen.

To be able to hear him and myself
to respond in honest ways
based on each other's conduct and treatment
to measure our sweet justice to each other
a balance between my own woman and my man's man.

I suppose all women must choose
to accept, to rebuild or to demolish
the moon house.

As long as we have the choice
our response ushers
in ease, equanimity.

I understand that waves do not move individually.
They overlap, fold into each other.
Rise and fall in a pattern.

I have not found it yet.

I take a shower.
The streaming rivulets
smash against the white tile floor
in beautiful violence,
become
gleaming translucent portraits
of splitting.

How to couple and maintain
whole?

The moon hovers
above to help us
find the way
over and over again.
A slice of my bones
floats light and round.
In her slow careful steps
across the sky
she continues on her route
and so do I.

AND WHAT OF THIS REVOLUTION?

1.
The cost of bread is too high.
Women want to drive.
People want to think.

Just give them smart phones
and revolt will follow.
The hand-held medium
carries the people.

What of other things unimaginable?

A river of humans in a plaza makes change begin.
Electronics extend into a thousand voices
connects the common current to a new way
to exist in an old world.

2.
There should be jobs.
There should be education.
It will not be fair.

3.
Walk farther out into the sea.
The raft ahead, the water only to your knees.
A mermaid changes her mind—
"What I thought is paradise is no longer."

4.
Can marriage work?
Will the woman be happy after twenty
years of knowing better?

Is the answer travel?
Or TV? Or eating key lime pie? Drinking beer?

Or being bold in hot tubs?
Or home improvement?

How do evolutions happen
each day and night?
The adaptations we all
make with each breath?

The angle of our bones
the way everything in the hammock
is elliptical and functional.

Of funneling rain water
to the limestone for survival.
The leaves, the saw grass
all function to live.

Does that mean we
need each other?
Are we the rounded
curves that take us through the edges?

5.
Your nose is both sharp and curved,
your mind the same.

The way you know me.
The way you appreciate me.
It is unprecedented.

Are you just lucky
or have the others been so incompetent?

You are so responsible.
This echoes of a revolution.

6.
Let's walk toward the unknown.
Like the young men who put

newspaper under their clothes,
let's wrap our bodies in whatever
protective armor we can.

7.
I take my memories
wrap them around me
a transparent shield to guard me
from the same mistake twice
but it never happens the same way.

8.
Memories are more like a guide, to cause pause, to study and then to move forward. Keep moving and keep your eyes even with the horizon.

My poets will not like these long lines. No one likes to wait their turn. I will revolt. I will write in gushes and languish in my own thought and welcome you to follow and seep and lose the thread for a moment and return when you hear that bell in your mind of crosshatching litanies.

Is this what change consists of? The cost of food rises. A man sets himself afire. One butterfly too many in the Everglades. Fires in San Diego. A chemical need that I try to satisfy in many ways. At some point it must stop. It must change.

9.
We all have our revolutions.

DISHWASHER FULL, DISHWASHER EMPTY

A leak in the back of my throat. A hole where I lose important things.
They slip away and there is nothing I can do but mourn the loss.

The retirement article. The one car key. My boyfriend. My velvet red
t-shirt. His note. All disappear. Leaving a pervasive sadness.
Constant like a too-tight dress that protects me, conceals me, dulls me.

I still have to fold clothes. Clean the kitchen. Put away laundry. Clean the
closet. Search for recipes and shop. And feel sad. I need time to sink into
this tepid bath and think about what is missing.

I want to cleanse. I want my life to be different because I am different.

Pain and difficult times and questions make change.
Nothing comes without provocation.
I will ask. I will not hide or be afraid.

Dishwasher full. Dishwasher empty. It will happen again and again.
I get excited when it's all clean and empty and then it just fills again.

Fill my heart. I know it will empty. Fill it so full that I can take the empty.

THE RELEASE OF KEY LARGO

We round the Tamiami Trail Bridge engulfed in thin blades of saw grass.
There are so many birds; particulates of feathers drape the air.
Ahingas perch boldly on the railing flashing iridescent green—

the mating shade of their pupils. We join the slow shallow grassy river's
flow over limestone into mangrove forests and bladderwart.
Mosquitoes, larvae, spatterdock—all point to the freshwater.

There is an underlying heat that strains to break through the cloud gauze.
The pace here is slower, the traffic fast. Gas is cheap and people like to drink.
I dreamt of my first home in Baton Rouge (peeling wallpaper, a dusty deep

red chandelier, leaded windows, still no termite contract).
It seemed like I owned it along with all the problems of the South.
The shoddy racist construction. The superficial gloss hiding serious flaws.

The piles of red-hot ants. That was long ago and so wrong.
Now is different. The practiced pace of the current.
How fish pivot back and forth, their centers silent.

Our vacation rental is on Adam's Cut—the only channel to the Atlantic.
The home, castle-like, faces the 1 freeway and an obnoxious purple sign
for Phantom Fireworks. It all seems unnatural. Boats parade by at night

when the current pulls in the opposite direction. Young men shine flashlights
hypnotizing crustaceans to rise. Shrimping, fried green tomatoes, and warm beer.
The cars continue to buzz past in another type of indifference.

Back home in LA it's raining. My boyfriend is in a deposition.
There is an agenda for a staff meeting. It goes on without me.
Something here makes me think. Being so far south and so flat

with such little elevation levels me. I keep thinking of our walk in
the Everglades. At the end of the wetland a crowd gathered and gawked.
We pushed ahead, waited and I stood on my tip-toes. A mass of twisted

alligators, as if wrestling and then held frozen in black mud. Hundreds. A ghetto
interspersed with vultures. A mix of scaled bodies and balding birds.
A boy sits down. A stranger kicks him. The dad says, "I told you to stand up."

Then the call with my boyfriend comes to mind, where he ended our
conversation with "thanks" as if I were a service—no one special—
how I dreamt of holes and leaks in my house in Baton Rouge.

Haunted by things left behind, unfinished. I want to finish them all.
I wish everything worked. I want to float down the current;
we all do and we all manage. We pause and we adapt. On the return

drive we pass a group of red water trucks spraying the sugarcane fields.
There must have been ten plumes with one hitting the road. As we drove
through the overspray, we crossed into the arc of a rainbow.

BODIES OF WATER

As a little girl
I stared at the
linoleum floor
watching its swirling golden borders
become ivory islands,
antique keys, and Abraham Lincoln's profile—
my mind recognizing familiar patterns
but not seeing myself.

~

I live richly on my own
with circles to wrap around people,
my supple curves
like butter melting in a skillet
one solid body to liquid
just the right golden-yellow for a moment.
A body of water seeking
equanimity
moving toward itself
spreading out.

~

Water rolls into thicker water in my brain
soothing, recalling
things to look forward to
peach pie
horoscopes
the white cat waiting on the stoop.

And then there are the days
of splitting grocery bags and spilling milk over
stucco steps like a white river of uncertainty.
Sweet chai iced tea also leaks into

the silvered cat water as a moth sinks down
dries in a salty crust in the corner of my eye—
reminding me the elements can at once be too much for me.
I continue anyway.

~

I am near the LA River
shallow with certain pollution
not certain of its function.
To be a part of its convergence
means to roil at times.
But, it is too difficult for you
to lift your head toward me and say
"Yes."

Or is it that I am just skinny dipping?
Wading into your lake
toes pointed, legs buoyant, full and plump.
Arms stroking and splashing until a tidal wave overtakes us
and it is too much.

~

I fear that it may be gone—
our waterway—
diverted from the times of freezer vodka.
The ridiculous notion of you in your underwear
simpatico with nature
running your hand across the horizon
tracing a wolf pack across the sky.

~

Until I realize we do this with each other
pretend we are someone else together—
we try to make it work but neither of us is ever happy.

~

Coming from behind pushing forward
plunging ahead
we go and go and go until
we no longer recognize ourselves
silver slippery liquid
holding no shape or meaning
other than necessary.

Until I see there are sister rivers,
offshoots, and springs
layers of water
full-bodied and knowing.

Mesmerized by a mermaid
fish tail flat against the reservoir.
Triumphant but somehow truncated, legless,
missing genitalia.

The water transforms her
pressing fins to legs
able to skip away.

How to Explain Loss

"Inhale, exhale, pause. You suspend, and in that suspension there is no pain. . . . These pauses add up."

—*Colleen Saidman Yee*

A CONVERSATION WITH PAIN

1.
I do not want you.
I know you too well.
You frighten me.

2.
May has been a month marked
by the end of possibility.

Of daisies rising from my chest,
then thistles.

Daisies in, thistles out.
Man #9 is an unreliable narrator.

3.
I see you recognize me.
You are a part of me
like a maligned left big toe.

I am careful with myself around you.
I want to feel all that you can tell me
but it's hard to endure
　　　　hot radish heat,
　　　　hand too rough, absent,
　　　　my name not called or mentioned.

4.
Man #6: Seattle, Space Needle pointing to the sky.
　　　　You don't want your picture taken.
Man #1: You don't want to join me in Palm Springs to visit family.
　　　　I go to the hospital and this new girl is near you, not me.
　　　　Your mom screaming she never liked me.
　　　　I believed her and I didn't.
Man #9: You telling me no one has loved you like I have.

Bend me, pull me, share your mind and take it away.
You do not pick me.

5.
Some people do not like me.
I am interesting, if sometimes beautiful.
An avocado, a kiwi, not necessarily a peach.

6.
I want the ability to wipe the sun out of the sky
absorb the gloom
and to stay with it because it exists in the familiar.

Let's not think,
or put it
in a secure pattern,
or hide it
in an obscure lacquer box.

Open. Look as your dark creeping
vines wrap into my spine
siphon energy, then cause a chemical reaction.
Slow me, exhaust me.
My body bigger with you.

7.
I take you into me,
Chew. You need
emulsion. Coat
my tongue.
Sweet cherry tart, too oily.
Need water; no, milk; no, let you fester.
Bubble up,
the offerings, bitter,
teach me to open slowly.

With a mango's sheen you slide down
my throat.
My mouth forms a wide circle,

an umbrella closing
around the emptiness,
an empire left behind.

Man #9's Monday morning exit at 7:30 a.m.:
"I am going back to my ex, so cancel the trip."

Never to know
the exotic woods of his home.

A person curled up
in the caves of my mind
for a month
then extricated himself.

Doesn't matter.
He is no longer here.
Just you.

8.
I am relieved.
I know you.
You are a constant.

9.
A garden growing. A white cat. Sun inside. A no. 2 pencil.
An ice cream on a Santa Monica beach with my blond niece.
She thought #9 was creepy.

10.
My four chambers are now thickened. Calcified to bone.
A solid case of protective coating to break open.
Thank you.

11.
Miniaturized into my hemoglobin
men walk into an artery,
vaporized from words and visuals and snake oil.

They explore the separate chambers,
feel the contraction coming just before my
valves open and shut.

Test out the options and features.
Recline along the
velvet contoured chambers.

"A mistake."
#3 said sorry too many times.

#9 expelled.
In a whoosh.
Closed. Not welcome.
Sealed. Shuttered.

12.
I can take anything from you for two minutes.

13.
I wanted to travel.
I wanted the journey. Still do.

We meet on the way up.
Part on the way down.
Twelve failures.
Who's counting?

14.
My father's face, a map of mistakes.
How to find them,
live them, be them.

I see myself in him. Failed marriage.
Roaming mind. Stubborn. Certain we are
appealing. Hoping for the next.

But, after so many numbers,
I wonder if it is me?

I take you in, offer you some
spicy tea, pomp and circumstance.

I see you have glossy eyes, needs,
a certain grace and evenness.

I offer you a refill and you refuse.
I take more
because
when I feed you,
spend time with you,
I am numb, but not flat;
my mind festoons in agony
revealing interior landscapes.

Let me know you.
Let me keep you near.
You are the certainty
I mistakenly seek in men.

BLACKBIRDS

4/17
Longing is a framing for a question.
Decisions are in answers.
Change may always include
coalesce
separate.

4/19
Spring releases
mustard weed
reaching out with
green arms,
yellow blond heads
bobbing
wanting.

4/26
There is a rip
in my fine fabric.
Fix my eyes
to the moment of the flaw.
Hold them steady,
endure
the change.
I did not want—
it is just a tear, I am safe, I am here.

4/28
This morning,
as always, the blackbirds
sing on the telephone wire
as if nothing happened.
Everything is different for me.
So reassuring to see the wire
just as tense and forgiving
as they land or fly away.

MOSS

A tremendous relief. Walking with dogs and realizing
the difference between hope and disillusion.
That wildflower, the sun, landed face up
next to a path that leads nowhere.

The green hills dotted with yellow,
the prancing black dog, silver dog,
both aware of only what they notice.

You there in the clouds,
hovering just above still snow-capped peaks,
distance is the reason between us.

I glimpse the olive moss hanging
against lime algae, dense and rich,
surges of life alluring in the shade.
You would agree nothing is as lovely as green
creating its own light.

Listen, I am trying to tell you something.
What do I want? More. Walks with dogs.
Why do I want? To fill the empty valley with us.
Why empty? Life has its vacantness.

Is it OK? Yes.
But you are no longer there, so I only think to you.

The mosses know what it feels like
to flourish amidst nothing
driven by need and function—
we outside this clean simplicity—

mud and tree bark watching.

OF LIGHT AND LOSS AND LEMONS

I feel the warmth of the sun
against the lingering disappointment
that you are not in my life.

I curl inside, tuck under, burrow
beneath tarnished skin—taking it all inside.

I grow a miniature lemon tree on my balcony.
I am amazed how the sun and water
continue to give me gifts.

I am drawn to lemons.
Neat slices float in my water.
They are little rounds of cheer. A brightness.

I see the sun for myself,
as doors in a hallway,
unopened, each one standing, waiting.

Being alone in this pause
takes patience, a tree without blooms.

I mourn the loss of who I felt I could be with you.

The traditional wife.
Living in an elevated home on a hill.
We could share your child.

That idea of me is gone.
Fabricated in another language,
from some other borrowed life.

I am glad to be back in my own life
in my apartment.
Thirsty, I pour a glass of water.
I want to add a squeeze of juice,

head out to the balcony and count
seven new green globes on my dwarf
Meyer tree. Plus, three yellow-and-white star blossoms.

And one perfectly ripe and heavy lemon.

OUT OF THE BLUE

for Jenny Faith King and Christina Rivera

They met in a bar
burning a path through the air
years after college
brilliant white-blue flash
to find love beyond love beyond lightning.

it reaches down for us
an erratic charged path
between clouds and earth

The couple races ATVs,
two friends trailing,
along a shore in Costa Rica
stretching into the future.
strike path not predictable

The sky suddenly splits—
bright collapses into dark.
we are electrical beings
Laughs tuck into their throats; they
swerve toward
the shelter of a tree.
in a state between meaning and chance
The lead rider, her dark coils spiral in the wind,
is more who she is than ever.

She fixates on the feathery canopy as
they huddle to wait out the storm.
She notices a nearby metal awning,
a bus stop overhang, obscured by their tree.
bolt temperatures run hotter than the sun
"Is it safe here?"
The thick humid drops smack against the leaves.
"Aren't we supposed to avoid trees in a storm?"

clouds charging

"Should we get back on the quads?"

Jenny with fair hair confesses,
"I'm scared."
path of least resistance

A thickening of air
something missing
internal vibration; discord,
you know to run.
animal instinct
You have to protect yourself.
the current will flow through you, pass through your body, change you

Christina jogs back to her ATV,
hops astride its black rubber tires and
sudden massive flow of electrical current
flings a droplet from her nose with a jerk of her neck
tens of thousands of volts
shoot up her right leg and arm
her body loops to the right
like a rope
recoils, straightens, then
turns to see her two friends and lover
sprawled in irregular patterns across the ground.
air breaks down
They are further apart than before.

Their love was always catastrophic. Gigantic.
She tries to revive her Jenny for an hour.
ions positively and negatively charged
Her own heartbeat silent in another body
pumping, pulsating and thrusting
to push the life back into her.
the conductive path
Curls asunder, her right shoulder trembles.
Jenny's dense chest remains hollow; she does not rise.
Her body thickens as rain and blood pools.
the moment after a strike glows lavender

Each question opens another chasm
expanding the gap opened by
lightning's erratic path,
twiggy electric arm of a sky witch,
energy, pulses of energy.

The natural world offers relief until it strikes you down.
Storm chasers, people on vacation, friends, the Yoruba people
in the lightning capital of Rwanda
who know existence can change in an instant.
A survivor says it "feels like dying for 28 minutes and going to heaven."

a cloud burdened with contrast must release the friction
seeks the ground to neutralize the charge
The human body produces streamers reaching for the oncoming electricity
purple flags attracting
the current.
air becomes so hot it explodes into thunder and shockwaves

She sees damp sand
smells the singe but can see no smoke.
Reliving that incongruous instant
her right arm throbs,
swells with the same humidity.

Another survivor saw his friend struck at summer camp.
He continues to wonder about random violent occurrences.
there is a leader path; then the bolt follows the same route
"I cannot accept that it happened for a reason,
nor can I really accept that there is no reason."

Shango—god of fire, lightning and thunder
swings a double-headed axe of destruction,
reminds us the only way to carry on is to be humble,
in awe of what we do not understand.
swing to the extreme for an instant

The world is full of strange events.
These things happen, Paul Auster knows, and that is their only meaning.

Except the lightning holds on. Contours his thoughts. He continues to write about the search for meaning.

Keep your feet close together and lower to the ground
in a ball. Do not touch the earth with your hands or head.
Do not lie down.
Christina was saved because her feet did not touch the earth.

The randomness of loss makes it seem personal.
Accidents are the beginning of something.

She keeps looking for Jenny in the horizon. Each night she walks the beach, gazing toward heaven, or just a little lower, to see her Jenny in the sunset. Christina's rust-brown eyes with an aura of gold follow the purples, pinks, blues hoping to see in the dark outlines of Jenny in the clouds.

The indifferent skies.
There is no translation.
Christina's voice calling for Jenny integrates with other sound particles.
Dissipates.

A healer told her to turn away. Turn from the sunset and face the darkness. She will never find Jenny in the disappearing light. She needs to look into the night, into the evening dark, and face what cannot be faced—the loss of Jenny. This will take her to Jenny. Being in the world alone. No one, nothing else offers comfort to this immeasurable emptiness, a hollow cone that only narrows. The darkness will lead to Jenny.

Here among us are the dead, the half-dead,
the ones who have seen the worst and survived,
who swallow pinecones, tar, aluminum cans.
Loss opens at the seams
turns bodies inside out
stretches skin around another
because that person cannot stand to be the one who lived.

flash of light marking the end
The randomness.
Dead at 36.

streaking across the sky
energy combustion collision

See the edge and bring her
back a glimpse of death
that cold conductionless moment
the echo of nothing
the silence of atoms at rest, bones sinking.

There is a lapse, inexpressible.
The space between the strike
leaves
what is what happened
and what feels like a secret inside a disseminated body.

Why now amongst such happiness, such levity, such hope?
The horizon pulled thin
transparent
no boundary between sky and earth
it never takes a direct path
the loss wide and immense
no one can know
it all burned down the center of her
waiting for Jenny to come in and lie down here inside her.

The question will never be quiet.
One life evaporates, a vacancy
that leads to more loss
more gaps between air
thoughts, words, understanding.

Christina is not the same person. She is nothing like she used to be.
"We are many people; events bring different sides of us forward."

The woman with curls is numb when she thinks of the moment. Her right arm holds her midsection in protection. She has to convince her body to release her arm. "It's OK. We are safe now. Relax, go ahead, straighten down my side. It is OK now. Release."

She seeks healers. Body workers. Meditation. Séances. Card readings. Daily trauma therapy. All the messages are the same.

Complete the process.
Complete the incomplete.

Discharge the energy.
Let it go.

Strike.

Set the force free,
release it from your body,
from your tissues.

Send the energy away.
Be like lightning.

Be like an animal after it's hunted,
and then escapes.

Shake your body,
twist your skin
to send all the forces
that just saved you
away from you
so you can continue to live.

The healing begins with each
intake of air, each gasp,
then release.

Take in.
Give back.

Absorb.
Return.
Fill.
Empty.

Blow the pain into the current.
Take it back in.
Give it back.
Inhale take.
Exhale give.

This exchange
over and over—
beginnings and ends.

Lie across the horizon, surf the undulations of heaving chests,
falling suns, restless waters. See aching bodies in how the
waves curve forward, throw themselves to the shore.
Welcome that darkness; note how your body trembles
from experiencing the impossible.
Recalibrate. Follow the needle back home.
Your spine now twines two cords; your heart
feeds four arteries. Your electric mind grows
more flexible with each breath; humanity
moans and swirls in your tissues.

TECOLOTE WINTER WALK

Mist spits in my face as I plunge ahead.
There is no one around.

How can I get so easily lost in my own life?

The path and the dog guide me into the canyon along
old-man eyebrow grass and spent vines alongside new growth.

The surviving green calls out for more light, more oxygen, more life.

The dog races between the tall reeds, like a show dog, cutting "s" paths.
The dry grasses rub under her belly releasing joy and abandon.

I walk calmly behind her and smile at her madness.

The same must be true for people and dogs.
The surprises come from beneath and within.

It is the holiday finally and bright red berries pop against evergreens.

On this December morning, where rain is rare, I see a single
white flower in winter, as if snow blooms from the ground.

FOR MY SISTER

In your leaving
I see our family home slide toward Tecolote Canyon's edge
tilting open to glimpse into the collapsed wreckage that is our lives.
We watched the two of them, mom and dad—
he pontificating and wanting a salute,
she only listening.
It can be better to be alone.

Alone seems safe.

I loved everyone so deeply,
        pushing mom as she mowed the lawn,
        bringing dad bowls of potato chips or saltines
so warmly,
in that house surrounded by gorge and dogs, our dogs.
I remember our green-speckled and ragged linoleum, the moment I knew
we were poor,
that we were different,
less than the neighbors
with their gleaming floors.
So, I remain partially mute
speaking of summers of Slip 'n Slide, watermelon and corn dogs.
The constant bee sting of poverty and loss
for fear it exists
inside me.

~

Is it like this for you, too, my middle sister?
I can only see life as I want to see it.
But you see it all, don't you, middle girl?

~

I am no better or different from our parents.
Built from their breath and touch
they live here in me and I live between them.

Last week, I drove by a random house under construction
        and the architecture inside me collapsed.
        The tearing-down-need for my own home.
        My own longing for structure
        reaching up and out and falling on me.
I paused and stayed with the sway
of destruction and let it take me back to our tiny cottage
at the end of the street.
Tumble.
Toward.
Vibrancy and freedom in owning my own damage.

~

The recognition that our lawn, contouring gracefully around the sidewalk
dry and brittle in spots
is the yard my father and I dug up fifteen summers ago,
we tilled
and we bent and we raised
a thousand times
to install an intricate system of faulty sprinklers.
Flawed with loose connections and sealed in our sweat.
Brown spots remain.
I am both distressed and unfazed by my sister's leaving.
She is my home,
my incarnation of place.
Gone to Montana all of a sudden.
Is she making it up the stairs to bed each night? Can she and her family
drink that orange well water? Will the white fence hold it all in?

~

She is not gone.
She is radiance; she is my love.
My mom cannot talk about it. My dad thinks
he's been too harsh, misunderstood.
Deep in the center of my chest
I hold you here, sister.

The butterfly of my ribs, the openness and the closeness —it is here I
sense you;
you will not
leave.

You balance between my ribs,
host the red barn of my heart.
You fling open the double-door and stride through
a hitch in your gait but steady movement through me.

~

I will see you. In Montana. In September. Just like you are here.
Sister. Sister.
And into the splitting we go to find ourselves
        canyon erosion, mudslide
mangled and needy and torn up—
I am not this plastic thing.
This thing, this likable thing.
No. I can be unwelcome and desperate, a famished deer in your garden.
So afraid that life is slowly moving away from me.
And I cannot grasp it, but I see it leaving.
So I went away.
Baton Rouge to Los Angeles.
Away for ten years, lost in Spanish moss and Southern California's glow.
I traded myself for a few things seeking happiness.
Now I gaze into our old home, splitting open, calling me back
to join its song of abundance paired with a chorus of "not enough."

~

Sister, show me the grace to understand
that this is not who I am; it is where I come from.
I feel your hand, sister, hovering over my sternum.
Your almond palm waves over my convulsing chest
like a magician waving her wand over my stiff body, transporting me,
softening me, transcending the idea of me, bringing me back.
You ask me again and again, "How are you?"
Reminding me of who I am beyond what has happened.
I awake and I want to empty my bedroom

paint it in elegant blues
and silvers with simple touches from the ocean.
Then tend my garden, a balcony garden with a lemon tree.
My own space, in water and in life, my home.

Let us quell the destructive
current that runs between my heart and chest
turns my body against myself
in monolithic channels between the moon and my bones.

Instead of interruption, let us sway,
sister, our heads tipped back in the pool,
our blond hair fanning out
moving with the currents
in a dance with the ripples of how things are—
undulations of tiny destructions
layer over waves of vibrancy—
and here we remain, holding place in the current.

OF HEAVEN AND EARTH

As the Pacific Surfliner train hurls me north
from San Diego into LA

I look out my darkening window,
gaze upward to gauzy clouds backlit in gold.

No one else seems to notice
how the sinking sun's eye beams down,
reads the cumulous as incandescent

text, absorbs it, and sends the wisdom
wide across the horizon in vaporous script:
        "Change, change me, change us, change."

I see the cluster of clouds as
steam dragons ascending to heaven, calling to each other—
        "Arise through openings.
        We cannot be contained.
        Release the vapors of our bones, thoughts."

These noble cumulonimbus,
growing ten miles high, cry out—
        "Conversion begets us."

We pass Oceanside as dusk
reaches down to touch a thousand fish on their triangle heads
igniting an iridescent ocean urging them—Glow. Swim. Live.

The waves roll to the south and birds
indiscernable black dots raise as a flock when the train passes,
join sky, water and sand.

Cumulus puffs whisper welcomings to all of this mutability,
        "There is no distinction between us, waves, and ocean.
        We are too close to exist on our own."

Ephemeral, the shapes continue to change,
they allude to disappearance,
instability and being left unfulfilled.

"Let it go," they sing in chorus.

We all hang on the verge of evaporation,
interacting with the elements,
just part of the water cycle.

Distant cirrus, made of ice crystals,
demand their own dissolving into water.
They chant in drops of liquid bronze.

Night welcomes their sense of anguish,
of missing elements, disappointments.
We can best see emptiness at night.

The ocean absorbs all
in her expanse of blue agitation
to cleanse and to release again in the morning

and we will begin again. Thanking the rhythm
of the aqua, pearl and yellow guides. Tomorrow
there will be even more birds in the sky to confirm it is true.

The train banks north into evening,
entering a bruise.

I turn around, crane my neck backwards,
not ready to leave the sunset, the water, the clouds or the horizon.
But the imaginary surface is just that and it is time to move forward.

Everything rises in the east.

I am just as capable of renewal as the sky, as the clouds.
I am formed of it and I am surrounded by it.

The nebulae return to us on dewy nights
the equivalent of

watching our bodies rise in vapor
and fall again in steam.

Light catches these droplets
and changes them into
glowing lanterns.

The answers
adorn eyelashes
in dew—
blessings
for transformations.

Acknowledgments

I give thanks to the intrigue of pain, of loss and of the missing as well as the reassurance of sunlight, love, mountains and the compassion of others, all that keeps me writing. I thank my mom for my love of sitting in the sun on the edge of our canyon. When I write, something compels me forward and I never know what will be revealed. This reminds me of my father and our coffee breaks. It is my sisters, my proud smart survivor sisters, who reach for me (and my poetry) with open arms. I could not survive without your endless love and insight. In my next poems I will concentrate on feeling—thank you Susan Seeck. I most enjoy being aware and for this I credit Diana Winston's wisdom and openness. Thank you so much, UCLA, for establishing MARC to guide me to be in my own life. Thank you, Laura, for honoring touch and for the light in your eyes. In gratitude to Petrina for guidance. Kristin for inspiration. My girlfriends, Jana and Stephanie, you are my life sisters. My soccer women, you are my sister family. I am who I am because of the water bodies and canyons of San Diego as well as its community of smart and forgiving people who know how to absorb paradise. Baton Rouge and New Orleans instilled a love of Tony Chachere's spices, romantic Spanish moss and wooden homes as well as appreciation for taking things slow. LA offers everything so it introduces a diversity of self, of beauty and of culture. And oh the hidden places, the textured things to do, and the food! Thank you Cynthia and Jon for your canal house where I do a lot of writing. I would not be a poet without all the teachers who lent me their experience so I could continue on. Thank you, Ms. Ramsey, for the freedom, Rae Armantrout, for the expansion, Marilyn Chin, for the love of the story and, Glover Davis, for the gift of form paired with patience and kindness. Sandra Alcosser taught me the importance of lists of wild grasses. SDSU's MFA program continues to give me a community of writers. I thank the heavens for Chris Baron's generosity, Cali Linfor's well of humanity, and Heather Eudy's road map. It would be so difficult without you all and with you it is joy. I appreciate the men and the loss of them that forms the background to my inquiries. And for those of you who remain, my heart for your bravery. I grow from the steady presence of strong and giving women in my life. I also thank UCLA for providing all that is needed to produce excellence. Especially Cynthia and Gina. I value every person, every student, and every rich moment that makes me whole. Thank you all for getting me to the other side, no longer as hindered by my own self. I will not be able to do everything, but it will be enough. My gratitude fills the air to give back to each tree, bird, and cloud—all that takes my breath away. I celebrate the forces in our world—water, gravity and energy—all that lives within us changes us.

Notes

Pacific Standard Time shares its title and loose overlapping concepts with a major California art retrospective involving several Southern California galleries and museums showing seminal works of the 1970s–1980s.

The definition of "lacuna" is from Dictionary.com, and the poem's concepts are inspired by UCLA German 59 course readings.

I thank Writers Anonymous for "Union Station."

I appreciate Diana Winston's help with exploring the Four Graces concept in "Four Graces: A Blessing for the World."

I am indebted to Christina Rivera for opening her pain and sharing her loss of Jenny with me and the world. Christina, you offer such grace and such love. Thank you for helping me understand what is incomprehensible.

"Out of the Blue" descriptions of lightning inspired by "How Lightning Works" http://science.howstuffworks.com/nature/natural-disasters/lightning.htm.

Some event details in "Out of the Blue" are from *The Acorn*'s "Woman Killed in Lightning Strike Led Active Lifestyle" by Anna Bitong and "Lightning Kills Westlake Graduate in Costa Rica" by John Scheibe from vcstar.com.

"Out of the Blue" lightning survival stories and quotes from *Act of God,* a film by Jennifer Baichwal.

"Of Heaven and Earth" cloud knowledge and inspiration came from two *Los Angeles Times* articles, "Poetic Wonders" by Liesl Bradner and "With Heads in the Clouds," an essay by Reed Johnson.

Chris Baron

was born into the tumultuous life of an artist's family. He is passionate about the importance of art as a practical resource for discovering truth and as a means of survival in our everyday lives. He completed his MFA in Poetry at SDSU in 1998. Baron has published numerous poems, essays, and articles in magazines, anthologies, and journals around the country, performed on radio programs, and participated in many readings, lectures, and panels. He has been fortunate to travel widely. Baron served for thirteen years on the executive board for the Border Voices Poetry Project. He works with the CS Lewis Foundation, Musalaha, and many other professional and social communities. Baron is a Professor of English at San Diego City College where he is the director of the Writing Center. He also works with local high schools and other organizations on education reform. He lives with his wife, Ella, and his three wonderful children on a hidden mountain in San Diego where someone only needs to speak "friend" and enter.

Heather Eudy

was born and raised in San Diego County amid scrub oak, rocks, red-shouldered hawks, and pomegranate trees. Always restless, she left for Colorado upon graduating high school, then for San Francisco to study writing as an undergraduate student, and wound up in San Diego again working construction until pursuing her MFA in Poetry at San Diego State University. After completing graduate work, she got a job delivering cars cross-country and later made southern Mexico her temporary home. She is now Professor of English at Southwestern College in Chula Vista, California where she teaches composition, literature and creative writing. Her work has been featured in several anthologies. She continues to travel widely.

Photo: Susan Tidey

Cali Linfor

lectures in Rhetoric and Writing at San Diego State University. Her scholarly work focuses on issues of educational equity. Linfor moved to San Diego to attend graduate school in 1996 and never left. She is honored to be a member of the Mayday Poetry Workgroup along with the other poets in this book. Linfor's publications include poems, articles, and short stories. She served as poetry editor of *Epicenter Literary Magazine* for sixteen years. Linfor was born in Garden Grove, California in the 1970s. She grew up mainly in Riverside, California. Reading and writing were a struggle for her as a child being both dyslexic and having been born with no opposable thumbs. But, convinced of the power of words, she eventually received a BA from UCLA in English while studying under Paula Gunn Allen and graduated with highest honors. She also has an MFA in Poetry. She lives happily near the banks of the San Diego River and the rolling hills of Mission Trails Regional Park with her family.

Sabrina Youmans'

Photo: Caroline Martens

byline has graced magazines and newspapers. For the last 17 years, she has returned to the university to teach students and student-athletes about writing and learning at SDSU, LSU, and UCLA. She earned her MFA in poetry from San Diego State with *Pockets of Air*. Youmans views poetry as a vibrant and spiritual act of engagement that confronts moments of brutality to seek insight, pleasure and transcendence. She continues to see loss as her muse and wonders if the clarity that misfortune brings can be achieved in other ways, without the devastation. This is her first book of poetry. A San Diego native, Youmans grew up with Tecolote Canyon as her backyard. She currently resides in Los Angeles but remains tethered to San Diego and all its trappings of paradise.